Farmwise

Your essential guide to health and safety in agriculture

London: TSO

a Williams Lea company

Published by TSO (The Stationery Office), part of Williams Lea, and available from:

Online
www.tsoshop.co.uk

Mail, Telephone, Fax & E-mail
TSO
PO Box 29, Norwich, NR3 1GN
Telephone orders/General enquiries: 0333 202 5070
Fax orders: 0333 202 5080
E-mail: customer.services@tso.co.uk
Textphone 0333 202 5077

TSO@Blackwell and other Accredited Agents

Printed in the United Kingdom for The Stationery Office
J003467086   c4   11/19

Acknowledgements

Thanks to the following organisations for their help in providing images:

AGCO Limited
CLAAS (UK) Limited
Collinson plc
Hereford and Worcester Fire and Rescue Service

Contents

Foreword

Since *Farmwise* was first produced, in 1992, it has reached a wide audience in the agricultural industry. This latest edition continues to provide practical advice and guidance to help you achieve good standards of health and safety – and reduce injuries and ill health.

The persistently high rates of fatal incidents and work-related ill health in the industry are of real concern to HSE, the representative industry bodies and many farmers. HSE is continually working to use new technologies and innovative methods of communication to improve, target and deliver key health and safety messages and guidance to those working in the industry.

Injuries and illness can ruin lives and businesses. Solutions are often simple and cheap and the people best placed to make farms safer are farmers and their employees. Health and safety is a fundamental requirement of a sustainable farming business and should be regarded as an essential part of farm business management. Unwise risk-taking is an underlying problem in the industry and those working on their own are especially vulnerable.

I hope you find the time to read the sections relevant to you, your business or your place of work. HSE's efforts alone will not build a safer and healthier industry. It is for everyone in agriculture and the wider food chain to play their part. I hope this booklet encourages you to tackle health and safety in your workplace today and in the future.

Rick Brunt
Head of Vulnerable Workers, Agriculture, Waste and Recycling Unit
Health and Safety Executive

Introduction

In the last ten years, almost one person a week has been killed as a direct result of agricultural work. Many more have been seriously injured or made ill by their work.

This booklet has been prepared by the Health and Safety Executive (HSE) to help you to:

- effectively manage health, safety and welfare;
- comply with the law;
- carry out the risk assessments that you must do, eg under the Management of Health and Safety at Work Regulations 1999;
- work safely and healthily.

The guidance in this booklet is relevant to everyone working on farms, whether employer, employee or self-employed, and will help you identify the causes of injuries and ill health, eliminate hazards and control risks. The first part covers managing health and safety and is primarily aimed at those responsible for running the farming or horticultural business (partners, directors and sole traders) but will also be of interest to others.

The other sections cover specific risks in your industry and give you easy-to-follow, practical advice to keep you safe and healthy at work.

In this booklet:

- 'must' indicates a definite legal requirement;
- 'dos and don'ts', 'shoulds' and 'should nots' and other recommendations represent good practice to help you do what is reasonably practicable;
- 'think about', 'consider' and similar phrases contain a tip or hint which may not amount to a precise legal requirement but indicate an approach to a health and safety problem which ought to be considered;
- 'reasonably practicable' means that the degree of risk in a particular job or workplace needs to be balanced against the time, trouble, cost and physical difficulty of taking measures to avoid or reduce the risk. In other words, if you can show that a particular risk is insignificant in relation to the effort needed to reduce it, you need do no more;
- a 'safeguard' is a means of reducing risk to health and/ or safety.

The booklet forms the basis of health and safety advice for agriculture. You will find further advice in the series of Agriculture Information Sheets (AIS), as well as other, more general, HSE publications. Each section contains references to some of the other most relevant HSE publications. You can also look at HSE's agriculture website: www.hse.gov.uk/ agriculture.

1 Benefits of preventing incidents

People have a right to return home from work safe and sound. Good farmers and employers recognise the benefits of reducing incidents and ill health among their workers, and are aware of the financial and other reasons to aim for and maintain good standards of health and safety.

The personal costs of injury and ill health can be devastating. Life is never the same again for family members left behind after a work-related death, or for those looking after someone with a long-term illness or serious injury caused by their work.

Managing risks in a sensible way protects you, your family, your workers and your business and can bring the following benefits:

■ a reduction in injuries and ill health and the resulting financial and personal costs;
■ improved productivity, good morale and a happier, healthier workforce;
■ better farming practice to help develop a sustainable farming business;
■ the ability to carry out weather-critical operations at the right time;
■ reduced sickness payments and recruitment/training costs for replacement workers;
■ reduced loss of output resulting from experienced and competent workers being off work;
■ longer life for equipment and machinery;
■ less chance of damage to machinery, buildings and product;
■ lower insurance premiums and legal costs;
■ less chance of enforcement action and its costs, eg the cost of dealing with an incident and/or fines;
■ reduced risk of damage to the reputation of the business.

Injuries and ill health in agriculture

Farming is a hazardous industry. Farmers and farm workers work with potentially dangerous machinery, vehicles, chemicals, livestock, at height or near pits and silos. They are exposed to the effects of bad weather, noise and dust. The risks also include family members working at the farm and children living at the farm.

Agricultural work can also be physically demanding and the repetitive nature of the work causes a range of health problems, including severe back pain.

Around 430 000 people work in agriculture, which includes farming and use of the countryside. This is less than 1.5% of the working population, yet agriculture has one of the highest fatality rates of all industries and is responsible for between 15% and 20% of all deaths to workers in Britain each year.

The costs and causes of death and injury

The total annual cost of injuries (in farming, forestry and horticulture) to society is estimated at £190 million[1] and around two-thirds of that is due to reportable injuries (£130 million), with fatalities accounting for around another third (£55 million).

The most common causes of death are:

■ transport – being struck by moving vehicles;
■ being struck by a moving or falling object, eg bales, trees etc;
■ falls from height;
■ asphyxiation or drowning;
■ contact with machinery;
■ injury by an animal;
■ being trapped by something collapsing or overturning;
■ contact with electricity, nearly two-thirds of which involves overhead power lines (OHPLs).

Many more injuries are non-fatal. Less than half of reportable injuries across all industry sectors are reported each year; far fewer for agriculture, forestry and fishing. Surveys suggest that only 16% of the most serious injuries to agricultural workers, reportable by law, are actually reported. HSE estimates up to 10 000 injuries annually are unreported. Each one involves costs to the injured person and to the business.

The most common causes of non-fatal injuries are:

■ handling, lifting or carrying;
■ slip, trip or fall on the same level;
■ being struck by moving, including flying or falling, objects;
■ falls from height;
■ contact with machinery;
■ being injured by an animal.

People working in the industry can also be permanently disabled by ill health. Breathing in dusts, handling loads, being exposed to noise or vibration, using chemicals and working with animals can all cause ill health, with symptoms that can take years to develop. In some cases this can result in premature death.

Many do not consult their doctor unless seriously ill, so levels of ill health are unclear. However, in agriculture:

■ about 12 000 people suffered from an illness which was caused or made worse by their current or most recent job;
■ musculoskeletal injury (back pain, sprains or strains) is over three times the rate for all industries;
■ the number of people affected by asthma is twice the national average;
■ about 20 000 people are affected by zoonoses (diseases passed from animals to humans) each year.

Workers may be exposed to extreme heat, cold, high humidity and radiation from direct and prolonged exposure to the sun (all of which imposes stress on the worker). They may also be exposed to excessive vibration, noise, or may have to work in uncomfortable positions for long periods and handle a wide range of chemicals such as fertilisers or pesticides.

Following the advice in this booklet will help reduce the risk of suffering a work-related injury or ill health.

[1] Source: *Costs to Britain of workplace injuries and work-related ill health: 2010/11 update* HSE 2010.

2 Organising for health and safety

As farmers and growers, you use management systems to make

sure that crops and animals are kept healthy and productive, and to enable you to stay in business. You plan what to plant and when, assess the risks of diseases and other incidents that may spoil the crop or animal. You control any problems, monitor growth, decide when to harvest, and store products in a way that ensures they stay fresh. You also work out how successful you have been and come up with improvements.

Managing health and safety is no different – you need to manage it to make sure that you, your workers, family members and others are kept safe at work. This advice is aimed at directors and managers but should also help supervisors and owners of small businesses.

If you follow the five steps in this section they should help you to manage health and safety properly, comply with the law and protect your workers and your business.

Step 1: Set your policy

You need a policy to set out your action plan on health and safety to improve standards in the workplace. It must be in writing if you employ five or more people, and needs to be carefully prepared, well thought out, up to date and based on real commitment.

Your policy should:

- be specific to your farm;
- state your general aims for your employees' health and safety. You, as the employer, should sign and date the policy to show clearly your commitment to it;
- accept that overall responsibility for health and safety rests with you, as the employer;
- outline the various responsibilities particular people have for making the policy a reality;
- describe the systems and procedures in place for ensuring the health and safety of your employees;
- set out how you will let your workers know about it, eg by giving them a copy and checking that they follow the rules and instructions in it;
- be reviewed from time to time and revised if your organisation changes or there are new hazards;
- be supported by enough money, people and time to put it into action;
- influence all your activities, including selecting people, equipment and materials, and the way work is done.

Step 2: Organise your workers

To make your policy work you need to get everyone involved. There are four parts to this 'positive health and safety culture', based on good business management practice:

- **Communication**: Provide information about hazards, risks and precautions to employees and contractors; discuss health and safety regularly; and lead by example to let everyone know that health and safety is important.
- **Co-operation**: Consult your workers and any representatives; involve workers in planning how to do the work and review how things have gone, working out safe methods and solving problems.
- **Competence**: Assess the qualities and skills needed to carry out jobs safely, particularly for especially dangerous work; make sure all employees, including managers and temporary workers, are adequately instructed and trained; and arrange for access to advice and help.
- **Control**: Demonstrate your commitment and provide clear direction; identify people responsible for particular health and safety jobs; and make sure everyone understands their responsibilities and the consequences if they do or do not carry them out.

Step 3: Plan and set standards

Planning is the key to making sure that your health and safety efforts really work and involves setting objectives and standards, assessing risks (see section 3 'Risk assessment') and developing a positive health and safety culture.

Management standards are set to show how plans or actions can be consistently delivered. You probably set standards every day to achieve best performance yields on your farm.

Your health and safety standards will set out what people will do to make your policy work and control risk. They should identify who does what, when and with what result.

Step 4: Check how you are doing

You can check how successful you are in managing health and safety in two ways:

- Before things go wrong, by finding out whether you are achieving the standards you have set with regular inspection and monitoring. This can be with spot checks or thorough inspections.
- After things go wrong, by investigating damage to property, injury, ill health and working out why the standards were not met.

Step 5: Learn from experience

Monitoring allows you to review activities and decide how to improve performance. Audits, by your own workers or outsiders, can help you to see if your policy, organisation and systems are actually delivering the desired result.

Learn from your experiences and use what you learn from monitoring and auditing to improve your approach to managing health and safety. When you review your policy, pay particular attention to:

- how well you are complying with the law and any national standards that apply, eg British and European Standards for machinery guarding;
- how well you are complying with any management standards you set for yourself;
- whether you have identified anything missing from your health and safety arrangements that you may need to change or rectify;
- if you have achieved your objectives within given timescales;
- injury, illness and incidents and understanding the causes, trends and common features.

These indicators will show you where you need to improve.

Find out more

Managing health and safety: Five steps to success INDG275
Health and safety toolbox: How to control risk at work:
www.hse.gov.uk/toolbox

3   Risk assessment

What is risk assessment?

Risk assessment is a careful look at what, in your business, could cause harm to people, so that you can decide whether you have taken enough precautions or should do more. The law does not expect you to eliminate risk, but to protect people as far as 'reasonably practicable'. Taking action based on your assessment is what matters.

How do I assess the risk?

Follow these five steps:

Step 1: What are the hazards?

A 'hazard' is anything that might cause harm, such as working from ladders, or electricity. The 'risk' is the chance that someone could be harmed by these hazards.

- Spot hazards by walking around your workplace and watching how people work.
- Learn from experience. Think carefully about any past incidents or illnesses as these can help you pick out the less obvious hazards.
- Ask people who work for you what they think. They may have spotted something you have not noticed.
- Check the manufacturer's instructions for equipment or data sheets for chemicals to help you spot the hazards.
- Don't forget to think about long-term health hazards as well as the more obvious safety hazards.

Step 2: Who might be harmed and how?

For each hazard you need to be clear about who might be harmed, eg employees, casual workers, members of the public, contractors and family, especially children. Think about the more vulnerable people, eg untrained or new workers, expectant mothers, visitors and maintenance workers.

Work out how they might be harmed and how, eg being killed by a bale or vehicle, injured by falling through a fragile roof, or suffering long-term health problems from breathing in grain dust.

Step 3: Evaluate the risks and decide on precautions

For each hazard you need to look at what you are already doing, the controls you have in place and the way the work is organised, and compare it to what is needed to comply with the law. HSE's website (www.hse.gov.uk) contains lots of advice to help you do this. If there is a gap between what you are doing and what you should be doing, then you must take action.

For example, if you had an unguarded power take-off (PTO) shaft it would be no good to simply tell workers not to go near it. What you need to do to comply with the law is have a well-maintained and effective guard. In this case there is a big gap between what is in place and what should be in place. You would have to take action to install a new guard and then maintain it in good working order.

If you can, you must eliminate the hazard altogether, but if you cannot do this, then you must control the risks in the following order:

- Introduce a less risky option, eg switch to a less harmful chemical.
- Prevent access to the hazard, eg securely cover or fence a slurry pit or guard a machine.
- Organise work to reduce exposure to the hazard, eg put barriers between people and moving vehicles.
- Provide personal protective equipment (PPE), eg clothing or footwear.
- Provide welfare facilities, eg first aid and showers for removing contamination.

Step 4: Put the results into practice

A risk assessment is not an end in itself. It will not stop someone dying, being injured or made ill. This will only happen if you take action to deal with the hazards and risks you find.

If you find there are quite a few improvements needed, big and small, don't try to do everything at once. Deal with the most important things first, eg those that could kill, seriously injure or cause serious illness.

Make sure everyone who works on your farm knows about the results of your assessment and understands the controls you have put in place. Share information about hazards and risks with those who need it, eg tell contractors about asbestos in buildings.

If you employ five or more people then you must write down the significant findings of your assessment. Examples of completed risk assessments are on the HSE website: www.hse.gov.uk.

Step 5: Check controls stay in place and review the assessment

Regularly check your controls stay in place. You need to ensure you are still improving or at least not letting standards slip back.

No workplace remains the same. Sooner or later you will buy new equipment or change ways of working that might bring in new hazards. If there is a significant change you need to respond to it straight away and review your assessment.

Why not decide on an annual date to review your risk assessment, so that even if there have not been any significant changes during the year, you leave yourself some flexibility to anticipate change and ensure nothing is missed?

Find out more

Information on risk management at www.hse.gov.uk/risk
Health and safety toolbox: How to control risk at work: www.hse.gov.uk/toolbox

4 Consulting employees

What must I consult about?

Employers must consult employees on their health and safety at work. Where there is no recognised union, you can choose to do this directly with individuals or through representatives elected from the workforce, or use a combination of both.

You must consult about anything that could significantly affect employee health and safety, which includes:

- changes such as new or different procedures, types of work, equipment or ways of working, eg safe systems of work for sharpening knives on forage harvesters;
- arrangements for getting competent people (those with enough experience, knowledge and training) to help you satisfy health and safety laws;
- the best way to share information that must be given to employees. Consider issues of language, literacy and disability, if appropriate;
- planning health and safety training;
- the health and safety consequences of introducing new technology, eg new transmission systems on tractors.

What does consultation involve?

Consultation involves not only giving information to employees but also listening to them and taking account of what they say before making decisions. Your employees often know best about the health and safety issues in your workplace and how to deal with them.

You should tell them about:

- the risks and dangers arising from their work;
- what you have in place to control those risks;
- what they should do if exposed to a risk, including what to do in an emergency.

Make sure all employees, including those who have trouble understanding English, have understood the information you have given to them.

When should I consult?

There are no hard and fast rules about when you should consult or for how long, but it must be in 'good time' so employees have a chance to think about what you said before giving their views. There are also lots of ways you may choose to consult, eg with individual face-to-face discussion or weekly meetings. It is often better to have a simple way of consulting rather than something complicated.

What are the benefits?

Talking to employees about health and safety can result in:

- healthier and safer workplaces;
- better decisions about health and safety;
- a stronger commitment to putting decisions into practice;
- greater co-operation and trust;
- joint problem-solving.

Consulting recognised union representatives

Under the Safety Representatives and Safety Committees Regulations 1977 (as amended), a trade union can appoint safety representatives from among its members, each of whom has a particular function, including investigating hazards, incidents and complaints, and being consulted by the employer on health and safety issues.

Consultation does not remove your right as an employer to manage. You must still make the final decision, but talking to your employees is an important part of successfully managing health and safety.

Find out more

Consulting employees on health and safety: A brief guide to the law INDG232(rev2)

5   Contractors and family workers

If you are self-employed (meaning a person who works for

gain or reward other than under a contract of employment), whether or not you employ others, health and safety law places a duty on you to ensure the health and safety of everyone who may be affected by the way you run your business or do your work.

See section 9 'Building work' for information about how the Construction (Design and Management) Regulations 2007 apply to you if you use contractors for building work.

Contractors

Contractors are often used for particularly hazardous jobs, such as cleaning glasshouse roofs, repairing other fragile roofs, or cleaning out slurry stores. Some routinely visit farms, eg for seasonal work or for technical expertise, such as agronomists.

If you use contractors for any work, whether short-term, such as for silage making, or for major construction projects, such as building a grain store, you cannot simply tell them what to do and let them get on with it. Incidents may happen because contractors do not know about dangers on the farm or your workers do not realise that contractors are on site.

Selecting the contractor

When engaging any contractor, whether an individual or business:

- appoint the right people by assessing whether they are competent. Talk to them about their experience and skills in the type of work you want done. Ask neighbours who have used them about their performance. Check for evidence of appropriate pesticide or chainsaw certification (eg certificates of competence), or check their membership of a trade or professional body;
- check they have enough resources, such as people and equipment, to do the work safely;
- provide information they need to carry out risk assessments relevant to the hazards on your farm, such as where overhead power lines run, or risks from working in areas occupied by animals. You and your workers may be familiar with them, but contractors may not;
- check they understand the standards of health and safety management you expect of them;
- agree how you will co-operate and co-ordinate with each other.

Planning the work

If you want the job to be done properly it is worth agreeing beforehand exactly what is to be done, by whom, and how. Talk about the working arrangements with the contractor, in particular what procedures for safe working will be followed. Consider:

- safe systems of work generally, eg on fragile roofs, or separating people from moving vehicles in the farmyard;
- your own operations which may affect the contractor's work, eg the need for cattle to be brought into the yard where work is going on;
- what machinery and equipment will be used, eg are edges of ditches, dykes or slurry lagoons strong enough to support the weight of the machinery?
- what the arrangements for supervision will be. Make sure that someone keeps an eye on contractors on site and that they follow the safe method of working;

■ work that is particularly hazardous, where the safe method may be too complex for people to remember and should be written down. Method statements, permits-to-work or similar tightly controlled systems of work will be needed for tasks such as working in a confined space in a sealed grain or forage silo.

Make sure the contractor's employees understand your rules for safe working, as well as the hazards and precautions, and that you understand theirs. Each new employee coming on site should receive appropriate instruction and training and be made aware of the hazards in your workplace and any emergency plans, eg what to do if there is a fire.

Controlling contractors on site

Check what the contractors do on site and that they are sticking to the safe system of work they have told you they will follow. Keep them informed about hazards and changes to plans or systems of work which may affect health and safety. You need to make sure they are not put at risk by your work, and that they do not interfere with your safeguards. If there is a problem and health and safety standards are not being met, you need to find out why and take action.

Who is an employee and who is self-employed?

Workers will normally be considered to be your employees, irrespective of whether they are treated as self-employed for tax and National Insurance purposes, if working arrangements are consistent with a contract of employment. Among other things this means you:

■ tell them what time to begin and finish work, and agree their holiday periods;
■ tell them what jobs to do, how they should be done, and in what order;
■ provide the tools and materials for the tasks carried out.

If workers work mainly for your business, work in an agreed way, use tools and materials supplied by you, and are under your control then they will probably be regarded as your employees for health and safety purposes. If this is so then health and safety laws will apply to you in the same way as to any other employer. Employers have legal responsibilities to employees, eg in the provision of training and health surveillance, which they do not have for the self-employed.

The traditional 'self-employed' person or contractor who carries out work for you, such as silage making, can be easily distinguished – they will arrive, within limits, at their own convenience, pack up when they wish, provide their own work equipment etc, and devise a way of doing the job that best suits them. Someone who is truly self-employed will be in control of, and have a stake in, their business which they stand to lose should the business fail.

Family workers

Family workers may be self-employed, employees, partners, or directors:

■ If the business is a partnership and all those who work on the farm at any time are included in the partnership agreement, then each one will be regarded as self-employed.
■ If the business is a 'body corporate', in other words a company, then the company is the 'employer'. Directors and others working for that company may be 'employees' or 'self-employed'.
■ If the business is run by an individual trading on their own account then they are self-employed and others working for them may be 'employees' or 'self-employed'.

Just as with other workers, whether or not they pay their own tax or National Insurance may be irrelevant for health and safety purposes. If family members work mainly for your business, are told how to carry out the work, use tools and materials supplied by you, and are under your control then they will probably be regarded as your employees for health and safety purposes. This means health and safety laws will apply to you in the same way as to any other employer.

Temporary, casual and agency workers

If you use temporary, casual or agency workers, eg to carry out harvest work, you have a legal duty to ensure their health and safety while they are at work on your premises. Where workers are supplied to you by a labour provider, which may be a gangmaster or employment agency or business, you should:

■ agree with the labour provider who will take responsibility for health and safety management, supervision and training, providing and maintaining any personal protective equipment and, where appropriate, health surveillance. This can be covered in a written contract or service agreement;

- make sure each new worker is given information about hazards, the precautions in place and understands what to do in an emergency. Those new to a workplace and to the jobs to be carried out may be particularly vulnerable to harm;
- make sure the findings of any assessments, including risk assessment, are communicated to workers in a form they can understand;
- make arrangements for the health and safety of people who have little or no knowledge of the English language;
- check the worker has any special skills or occupational qualifications needed for the job;
- arrange for welfare facilities and accommodation where necessary.

It is an offence under the Gangmasters (Licensing) Act 2004 for farmers or growers to use workers or services provided by an unlicensed labour provider in agriculture, forestry and horticulture (as well as in other industries).

Employment agencies (who introduce workers to an employer they will work for permanently, perhaps on a short-term or fixed contract) and employment businesses (who place workers with an employer but keep a contract with them) have specific legal duties under the Conduct of Employment Agencies and Employment Businesses Regulations 2003 to provide information to the businesses that use their workers.

For more information, visit the following sites:

- Gangmasters and Labour Abuse Authority: www.gla.gov.uk;
- Association of Labour Providers: www.labourproviders. org.uk, and for employment agencies/businesses: www.gov.uk/employment-agencies-and-businesses/overview;
- HSE's migrant workers website: www.hse.gov.uk and its migrant workers and agency/temporary workers website: www.hse.gov.uk/vulnerable-workers/agency-temporary-workers.htm.

Lone workers

Lone workers are those who work by themselves without close or direct supervision. Putting in place safe working arrangements for lone workers is no different to organising the safety of other employees. When deciding on safe working arrangements, ask yourself:

- Can the risks of the job be adequately controlled by one person?
- Is the person medically fit and suitable to work alone?
- What training is required to ensure the person is competent and can work safely?
- How will the person be supervised?
- What happens if a person becomes ill, is injured, or there is an emergency?

Lone workers cannot be constantly supervised, but decide on the level of supervision needed based on risk, eg those new to a job might need to be accompanied at first. Put procedures in place to see they remain safe, which may include:

- someone in authority regularly visiting the worksite;
- regular contact by telephone or radio;
- automatic warning devices which operate if specific signals are not received periodically from them;
- checks that they have returned to their base after a task;
- access to a first-aid kit.

Find out more

Working alone: Health and safety guidance on the risks of lone working INDG73(rev3)
Using contractors: A brief guide INDG368(rev1)

6 Training and skills

Businesses achieving high standards of health and safety at work give a high priority to health and safety training as part of their overall management approach. Training in how to use other protective measures, such as guards on machines, PPE and safe methods of work, is vital.

To decide what training is required, you should take account of the capabilities, knowledge and experience of workers. They may also have particular training needs, for example:

- new recruits need basic training in how to work safely, including arrangements for accident reporting, first aid and fire;
- temporary or casual workers will be unfamiliar with the workplace and will be more at risk;
- non English-speaking workers will require information in a way they can easily understand. Check their understanding and monitor them to make sure it is put into practice;
- people changing jobs or taking on extra responsibilities need to know about any new health and safety implications of the work;
- young employees are particularly vulnerable to accidents, so their training should be a priority;
- some people's skills may decline over time, or bad habits may develop, so consider refresher training;
- new technology, equipment or machinery may require new skills;
- new, inexperienced or young employees need adequate supervision following training.

What is training?

Training can involve various methods, for example:

- instruction or on-the-job training delivered by experienced workers;
- sessions with qualified instructors or external trainers;
- attending local colleges or training centres;
- on a group basis or individually by personal tuition;
- computer-based or interactive learning.

To help you find out what is available, contact:

- Lantra, the sector skills council for the land-based industries;
- trade unions or trade associations;
- colleges of further or higher education;
- private training organisations and training providers;
- independent health and safety consultants;
- employer bodies (eg chambers of commerce);
- qualification awarding bodies such as City and Guilds NPTC or Lantra Awards;
- professional industry schemes;
- local health and safety groups.

Recognised standards of formal training and/or competence are normally required for using chainsaws, tree work, applying pesticides, all-terrain vehicles (ATVs), forklift trucks or telescopic materials handlers, sheep dipping and first aid.

Vocational qualifications (VQs)

These help you improve knowledge in a particular area, usually through a college or training provider, and focus on practical skills.

There are health and safety VQs specific to agriculture and horticulture available at two levels of ability, each level requiring up to 30 hours of study time. They will enable workers at all levels to:

- understand how incidents and ill health can affect both people and businesses;
- be aware of the main causes of incidents and ill health in the industry and how to prevent them;
- understand the key elements of the law and where to get information and advice.

For the self-employed or managers, VQs will also help them to:

- understand how to do risk assessments and tell workers of the outcomes;
- be aware of standards of training and competence for people in the industry;
- select contractors and work equipment to meet health and safety requirements;
- understand how health and safety fits in with the principles of good management.

For information on VQs see:
www.lantra.co.uk/awards/training-and-qualifications.
www.nptc.org.uk/qualificationdefault.aspx

Find out more

Health and safety training: A brief guide INDG345(rev1)
Rider-operated lift trucks: Operator training and safe use. Approved Code of Practice L117
Safe use of all-terrain vehicles AIS33(rev1)
Chainsaws at work INDG317(rev2)

7 First aid, emergencies and reporting

The law

The Health and Safety (First Aid) Regulations 1981 require you to have adequate arrangements for first aid. The Management of Health and Safety at Work Regulations 1999 require you to have procedures to be followed 'in the event of serious and imminent danger' – an emergency. The Reporting of Injuries, Diseases and Dangerous Occurrences Regulations (RIDDOR) require you to record and report incidents, diseases and dangerous occurrences.

In any business things sometimes go wrong. You need to be ready to deal with unplanned events and limit the damage caused. Think about emergencies such as serious injuries, fire, poisoning, electrocution, or chemical spills and plan for the worst that could happen. You may need a written emergency plan if a major incident at your premises could involve risks to the public, rescuing employees or co-ordinating the emergency services, eg where access into slurry stores or silos is needed, or if 25 tonnes or more of dangerous substances such as LPG or oxidising agents are stored.

Consider what could go wrong, and tell workers:

- what could happen;
- what to do, including calling the fire or ambulance services and shutting down plant;
- where to go to reach safety, or get rescue or fire-fighting equipment;
- how people (those in charge and others) will deal with the problems. Have you identified and addressed training needs and allocated responsibilities?

Check that:

- the emergency services have the OS map reference of your premises;
- you have marked the entrance of your site with a hazard warning sign and notified your local fire and rescue service if you have over 25 tonnes of certain dangerous substances on site, eg oxidising agents (such as certain ammonium nitrate fertilisers);
- you have emergency exits to allow workers, eg in grain stores, to escape quickly, and suitable arrangements to make sure that emergency doors and escape routes are kept unobstructed and clearly marked at all times;
- a competent person has been nominated to take control;
- you have adequate first-aid equipment and first-aiders;
- people are trained in emergency and evacuation procedures and have rehearsed what to do.

First aid

Immediately and properly examining and treating injuries may save life and is essential to reduce pain and help injured people make a quick recovery. Neglecting or inefficiently treating an apparently trivial injury may lead to infection and ill health. All farms must have first-aid equipment available, but what is appropriate for you will depend on the nature of your business and the types of incident that may happen.

You should:

- appoint someone to take charge of first-aid arrangements, including looking after the equipment and facilities and calling the emergency services when required. An appointed person will need to be available whenever people are at work;
- provide a suitably stocked first-aid container which is easily accessible in an emergency;
- provide information for employees on first-aid arrangements, eg notices telling people where the first-aid equipment, facilities and personnel can be found.

Also remember:

- In agriculture, a lot of work may be in places remote from emergency medical services, so provide travelling first-aid kits to be carried on tractors etc, or when particularly hazardous tasks, such as using chainsaws, are being carried out.
- If you employ large numbers of workers on site you may need to provide a first-aid room, a qualified first-aider, or someone with specialised first-aid training.
- Some substances can have serious effects on health, eg moisture-activated gassing compounds such as aluminium phosphide used for vermin control. All users should make sure they know the appropriate first-aid measures to take. Discuss medical treatment with your GP and consider the need for mobile phones or radios if they would reduce the time taken for the emergency services to reach a casualty.

What must be reported

If you are an employer, self-employed or in control of premises, you have a duty under RIDDOR to report some accidents and incidents at work. This duty covers everyone at work (including those on work experience and similar schemes) and non-workers, such as visitors, affected by the work.

Employers or self-employed people must notify the enforcing authority:

- immediately, of a death;
- immediately, of a reportable serious injury, such as a broken arm or leg, an amputation injury or where an employee or the self-employed person is seriously affected by an electric shock or poisoning;
- immediately, of a dangerous occurrence, eg where something happens such as a fire or explosion which stops work for more than 24 hours;
- within ten days, of an over-seven-day injury, where the employee or self-employed person is away from work or unable to do their normal job for more than seven days;
- immediately, of a death or major injury to a member of the public where they are taken from the scene of an accident to hospital;
- as soon as possible of any reportable disease or diagnosis.

Reportable diseases in agriculture include:

- most zoonoses (diseases passed from animals to humans);
- dermatitis from work with many products used in agriculture, including certain plants;
- asthma from exposure to dusts and animals;
- cramp of the hand or forearm because of repetitive movements.

Further details of reportable injuries and diseases are available at: www.hse.gov.uk/riddor

How to report

Online

Go to www.hse.gov.uk/riddor and complete the appropriate online report form. The form will then be submitted directly to the RIDDOR database. You will receive a copy for your records.

Telephone

All incidents can be reported online but a telephone service is available for reporting **fatal and major injuries only**. Call the Incident Contact Centre on 0845 300 9923 (opening hours Monday to Friday 8.30 am to 5 pm).

What must be recorded

You must keep a record of:

- any reportable death, injury, occupational disease or dangerous occurrence;
- all occupational accidents and injuries that result in a worker being away from work or incapacitated for more than three consecutive days. Although you no longer have to report over-three-day injuries, you must keep a record of them (you do have to report over-seven-day injuries – see above). If you are an employer, who has to keep an accident book, the record you make in this will be enough.

Find out more

Information on the RIDDOR Regulations can be found at www.hse.gov.uk/riddor
First aid at work: Your questions answered INDG214(rev1)
Basic advice on first aid at work INDG347(rev2)

8   Preventing falls

The law

The Work at Height Regulations 2005 cover all work activities where people could fall and injure themselves. The duties are on employers, the self-employed and others who have control over work at height. You must make sure work at height is properly planned, supervised and carried out by people who are competent to do the job.

Falls are the second biggest cause of death in agriculture. Those who survive may suffer broken bones or other serious injuries. Falls often happen from roofs, lofts, ladders, vehicles, bale stacks and unsuitable access equipment, such as grain buckets or pallets. These accidents and injuries cause you pain and cost you time and money. Most fall injuries can be avoided.

The law says you need to follow these rules, in this order:

- Avoid work at height where you can.
- Use work equipment or other measures to prevent falls.
- Use work equipment that minimises the distance and consequences of a fall.

Do not forget to check the safety of contractors working for you (see section 5 'Contractors and family workers'). Also see section 9 'Building work'.

Working on roofs

Fragile roofs are often the cause of deaths in agriculture. You must follow the hierarchy of the Work at Height Regulations 2005 and take steps to prevent anyone from accessing fragile roofs unless adequate means to stop people falling through them are provided.

Most types of fibre cement roofs (commonly known as 'asbestos' roofs, but not always containing asbestos) will be fragile. Roof lights will often also be fragile. No one must ever work on or from, or walk over, fragile roofs unless platforms, covers or similar are provided which will adequately support their weight.

Always consider first whether it is really necessary to access the roof. Does the work need to be done, or could it be done in some other way such as from below or from an integrated work platform? If you, your employees or contractors repair, replace or clean roofs, or access them for inspection or to get to plant, follow these rules:

- Plan the work.
- Set aside enough time to do the work.
- Take account of environmental conditions such as light levels, ice, wind and rain.

- Make sure everyone knows the precautions to be followed when working at height.
- Fix a prominent permanent warning notice at the approach to any fragile roof.
- Never walk on fragile materials such as asbestos or other fibre cement sheet, roof lights or glass. Roof lights and glass may have been painted over.
- Never 'walk the purlins' or 'walk the line of the bolts'.
- Roof ladders or crawling boards must span at least three purlins. They should be at least 600 mm wide and more when the work requires it.
- Don't use a pair of boards to 'leapfrog' across a fragile roof, but provide enough boards.
- Take precautions to prevent a person falling from the ladder or board. Use edge protection or safety harnesses, or safety netting where this is not feasible. Take specialised advice, but remember that harnesses require adequate attachment points and rely on user discipline and training to make sure that they are correctly used.
- Roof ladders must be securely placed, with the anchorage bearing on the opposite side of the roof. Do not rely on the ridge caps or tiles for support as they can easily break away. Never use gutters to support any ladder.

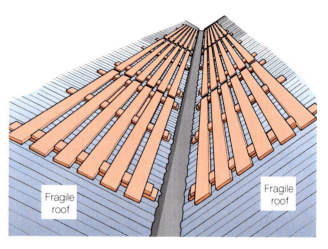

Permanent protection installed at valley gutter. (The protection should be supported by at least three rafters beneath the roof sheets.)

Working on or passing near to fragile roofing material

You will need to provide protection when anyone passes by or works nearer than 2 m to fragile materials, eg during access along valley gutters in a fragile roof, when an otherwise non-fragile roof contains fragile roof lights, or during access to working areas on a fragile roof.

You should:

- wherever possible, make sure that all fragile materials (eg 2 m or closer to the people at risk) are securely covered; or
- provide full edge protection (top rail, intermediate guard rail or equivalent and toe board) around or along the fragile material to prevent access to it. Make sure you take precautions when installing such protection, eg use appropriate netting.

If it is not reasonably practicable to provide such protection:

■ use safety nets or harnesses but make sure workers are trained and competent in their installation and use. If the building structure is unsuited to netting or harnesses (eg too low), a well-built and suitably sized bale stack close to the underside of the fragile roof being worked on will reduce the risk of injury if someone does fall through the roof.

Working on glasshouse roofs

Try to **avoid** working at height in glasshouses by, for example:

■ using automated roof cleaning and shading;
■ using mechanical washing systems or sprinklers;
■ reducing the need for cleaning, eg by managing leaf and other debris to lessen the need to clear blocked gutters;
■ considering safe maintenance when replacing or buying new buildings, eg positioning of motors;
■ avoiding high-level picking.

If you cannot avoid working at height, then prevent falls by planning this work properly.

If possible, reduce the risks by, for example:

■ stopping all production work activity below the area in which work is taking place;
■ using roofing materials less likely to be damaged, such as acrylic or polycarbonate sheets;
■ replacing glass from below;
■ examining glass sheets for flaws before handling them;
■ never working by lying directly on the glass itself;
■ never walking along a valley gutter without fall-protection measures in place.

If access onto the roof is unavoidable, safe systems of work will be needed:

■ Consider how, or if, airbags or staging could be installed below the work area. On new glasshouses it may be possible to install nets.
■ Use devices to help prevent falls when moving along, or working from, a gutter. If possible, use valley gutter protection such as timber bearers supporting runs of scaffold boards extending at least 1 m from the gutter on each side.

If the glasshouse will not support this weight, other equipment should then be used, such as:

■ permanent handrailing;
■ a taut line with harness;
■ ride-on trolleys;
■ lightweight balancing frames;
■ a combination of the above.

The equipment used will depend on the type of glasshouse, the width of the gutter and the job to be done. All equipment should be properly designed, constructed and maintained, and ride-on trolleys and balancing frames should be:

■ light and easily carried;
■ robust and strong enough to support the loads they will be exposed to, eg the weight of a person;
■ easily transferred from roof to roof without putting people at risk.

Be careful about snagging trouser legs on glazing bars. Tuck trouser bottoms into boots or socks or wear trousers with elasticated bottoms.

Glasshouse manufacturers should be able to give advice about suitable access equipment for particular glasshouse types, eg those with almost flush glazing bars, which can make positioning ladders etc difficult.

Getting on and off vehicles

You are more likely to be injured if you jump down from vehicles. Take your time climbing down from the cab and use the steps and hand holds provided rather than the steering wheel. Think about where you park and try to avoid potholes.

Loading and unloading

- Plan loading and unloading to avoid the need to work at height on the vehicle.
- Keep the load area tidy and as clean and free from mud and diesel as possible. Pick up loose ropes and straps. Check they are in good condition to secure the load and are safely stored when not in use.
- Wear well-fitting, slip-resistant safety footwear when working on vehicles.
- When buying vehicles, think about how you will be able to get to the high parts of a machine to maintain it safely. Ask for well-designed access, eg pick a vehicle where regular maintenance points, such as grease nipples, can be reached from the ground.
- Make sure that trailers are securely braked during loading and unloading.

Bales: loading trailers and stacking

Many incidents (some fatal) involve bales being loaded onto trailers, or during or after stacking. When loading, check that:

- trailer floors are in good condition and end racks or hay ladders are used;
- loads are built to bind themselves. Use sound bales for all edges;
- workers keep away from the edges. Drivers should indicate clearly before the trailer is moved;
- full loads are secured before leaving the field and no one rides on them. Provide ladders for access to the load.

Stacking is a skill, and requires competent people. Have you:

- provided training and selected fit people who are happy working at height?
- made sure bales are well interlocked, and sound bales are used for edges?
- instructed workers to avoid working near edges, and to keep away from loading equipment?
- considered guarding the edges of stacks in buildings by fencing in non-loading sides?
- provided ladders, secured in place, for access?

Inspect stacks regularly, and make sure destacking is carried out safely:

- Always take the top bales down first.
- Use handling equipment as much as possible.
- Avoid pushing bales off with your feet.
- Never pull bales from the bottom.

Falling bales regularly kill people, so keep clear when unloading or destacking.

Work platforms on forklift trucks

If you need to raise people above the ground, eg for building maintenance, use properly designed work platforms rather than ladders. Never use grain buckets, pallets, or other makeshift equipment. Serious injuries and death have resulted from buckets etc being accidentally tipped.

For planned or regular work at height, you should use a fully integrated and properly constructed working platform. This will have controls that are linked to and isolate the truck controls so that only a person on the platform can control the platform and truck movements. You should not normally use a non-integrated work platform (see HSE Guidance Note PM28 in 'Find out more').

- Only fit working platforms to suitable machines – normally forklifts with vertical masts or telescopic booms.
- Consult the manufacturer's/supplier's information to make sure that the truck and working platform are compatible.
- Only use working platforms on machines that have a tilt/trip 'lock' to prevent accidental tilting of the platform.
- Only use properly constructed working platforms fitted with full edge protection.
- Make sure any gates in the edge protection open inwards, upwards or sideways, and return automatically to the closed position.
- Make sure there are safeguards so that the person being lifted cannot contact dangerous parts of the machine (eg the lifting chains) with any part of their body.
- Do not climb on or over the guardrails.

Scaffolds

Many tasks will be less hazardous if you do them from a properly designed and erected scaffold. Use competent and experienced workers to erect a scaffold and make sure they are under the control of, and the scaffold is inspected regularly by, a competent person.

Check that:

- the scaffold is placed on level, firm ground with baseplates and soleplates, where necessary, properly braced with vertical supports (standards) every 2–2.5 m;
- the platform is at least 600 mm wide, with adequate supports, not more than 1.5 m apart;
- scaffold boards are tied down or overhang each end support by 50–150 mm;
- you have provided fall protection, eg guardrails and toe boards. The main guardrail must be at least 950 mm above the platform. There should not be an unprotected gap of more than 470 mm between the platform and any guardrail;
- there is safe access to the scaffold. Never climb the scaffold poles to gain access – use a ladder.

For mobile scaffolds, also:

- check the maximum recommended height in relation to the base dimension (including outriggers, if fitted). The base:height ratio is often 1:3;
- tie them to the building, or extend the base with outriggers;
- do not use in windy weather; always tie them if they are to be left unattended;
- clear the working platform of people and materials when the scaffold is being moved. Move it only by pulling or pushing at the base;
- wheel brakes must be 'on' and locked when the scaffold is used;
- do not overload the working platform or apply pressure which could tilt the tower.

Ladders

Ladders are not banned, but should not be the first choice if there is a safer way of doing the job, eg by using a scaffold or suitable working platform. If the job is quick (minutes not hours) and simple, you can use a ladder but always make sure that it:

■ has level and firm footings. Never use unsteady or slippery bases, eg oil drums, boxes, planks or an uncleaned animal yard;

■ is not placed against a fragile surface, eg fibre cement gutters. Use a ladder stay or similar;

■ is set at the most stable angle – a slope of four units up to each one out at the base;

■ extends at least 1 m above the landing place or the highest rung in use, unless there is a suitable handhold to provide equivalent support. Extending ladders should overlap by at least three rungs;

■ is secured against slipping, eg by tying both stiles to prevent slipping and rotation of the ladder or using a suitable stability device. Using a person to foot a ladder is not very effective and should only be a last resort.

When working from a ladder, try and maintain three points of contact with it at all times (eg both feet and one hand). Aim to keep both hands on the ladder as much as possible. Follow similar rules for stepladders and trestles.

Never:

■ use damaged or 'home-made' ladders – take them out of use and destroy or repair them. Check for defects regularly;

■ place ladders where there is danger from moving vehicles, animals, or electricity lines.

Inside silos or bins where grain loading will distort safety hoops, there are often fixed vertical ladders. Consider whether you need to access the silo at all. Can samples be taken from the auger? If you do have to climb or descend the ladder into the bin or silo, use a twin-tailed lanyard or suitable device to minimise your risk from falling and make plans for rescue in an emergency.

Tree work at height should only be carried out by competent people (see section 17 'Chainsaws and tree work').

Find out more

Case studies on HSE's agriculture webpages: www.hse. gov.uk/agriculture/experience/falls-from-height.htm
Health and safety in roof work HSG33
Working platforms (non-integrated) on forklift trucks PM28
Safe working with bales in agriculture INDG125(rev3)
Working on roofs INDG284(rev1)
Working at height: A brief guide INDG401(rev2)
Safe use of ladders and stepladders: A brief guide INDG455

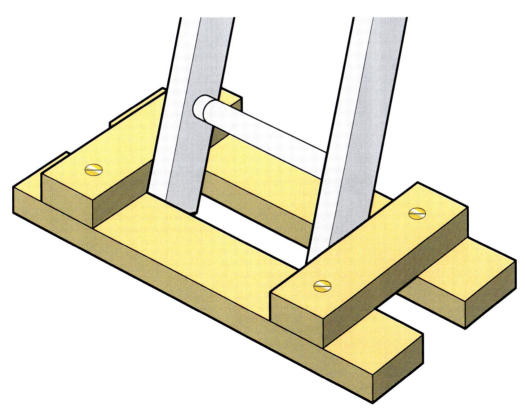

Secure ladders at the base to stop them slipping

9 Building work

For advice on working at height and the Work at Height Regulations 2005, see section 8 'Preventing falls'. Most farms carry out some building work, from dismantling and re-erecting entire buildings to dealing with asbestos. All such work involves risks and you must put proper controls in place.

Farmers are very resourceful and can often turn their hand to most things. Start by asking yourself if this is a construction job or a maintenance job and, in either case, if it is within your capabilities. If in doubt, consult a professional builder for advice.

Building contractors

If you are employing a contractor to do any construction work (including demolition) then the law imposes particular legal duties on you as a 'commercial client' under CDM 2015. A commercial client is any organisation or individual for whom a construction project is carried out in connection with their business or other undertaking (whether for profit or not).

The duties of a commercial client include:

- making suitable arrangements for managing the project, enabling those carrying it out to manage health and safety risks in a proportionate way;
- appointing the contractors and designers to the project (including the principal designer and principal contractor on projects involving more than one contractor) while making sure they have the skills, knowledge, experience and organisational capability;
- allowing sufficient time and resources for each stage of the project;
- making sure that any principal designer and principal contractor appointed carry out their duties in managing the project;
- making sure suitable welfare facilities are provided for the duration of the construction work;
- maintaining and reviewing the management arrangements for the duration of the project;
- providing pre-construction information to every designer and contractor either bidding for the work or already appointed to the project;
- ensuring that the principal contractor or contractor (for single contractor projects) prepares a construction phase plan before that phase begins;
- ensuring that the principal designer prepares a health and safety file for the project and that it is revised as necessary and made available to anyone who needs it for subsequent work at the site;

For notifiable projects (where planned construction work will last longer than 30 working days and involves more than 20 workers at any one time, or where the work exceeds 500 individual worker days), commercial clients must:

- notify HSE in writing with details of the project;
- ensure a copy of the notification is displayed in the construction site office.

You as a commercial client, the contractors and designers all have legal duties for health and safety that cannot be passed to each other by contract. This means you need to work with each other to make sure the job is done safely. Also look at section 5 'Contractors and family workers'.

Domestic clients

CDM 2015 now gives domestic clients certain responsibilities in relation to construction work. If you are having work done on your own home/farmhouse, or the home of a family member, and it is not in connection with a business, you will be a domestic client.

The only responsibility a domestic client has under CDM 2015 is to appoint a principal designer and a principal contractor when there is more than one contractor. However, if you do not do this (as is common practice) your duties as a domestic client are automatically transferred to the contractor or principal contractor.

If you already have a relationship with your designer before the work starts, the designer can take on your duties, provided there is a written agreement between you and the designer to do so.

Excavation

If excavating, remember:

- Trench sides may collapse suddenly whatever the nature of the soil.
- You need to decide before carrying out the work what precautions will be required to protect against collapse of the sides, eg shoring or battering.
- Keep a clear area around excavations to prevent people, materials or vehicles falling in, and the weight of soil or equipment from causing the sides to collapse.
- If you need to enter the excavation, provide safe access.
- There may be poisonous or asphyxiating gases in sewer openings, from marshy ground or from confined spaces (see section 13 'Workplace safety and welfare').

Keep well away from overhead power lines and underground services, including cables, oil and gas pipelines. Consult the utility companies or the pipeline operator before you start work to establish where they are.

Asbestos

Most farms have some asbestos-containing materials (ACMs), eg compressed asbestos-cement roof sheets, asbestos insulation board (AIB), cladding or rainwater gutters and down pipes. Asbestos can be found in boiler or pipe lagging, building partitions, preformed water tanks, ceiling and roof tiles and bitumen roofing felts. Remember it may also be found in fixed plant and machinery, eg insulation panels, gaskets or seals.

The Control of Asbestos Regulations 2012 require farm owners and tenants with leases that include the responsibility for building maintenance to carry out a survey of the premises to locate ACMs and record their condition. You then need to use this information to assess the risks from asbestos and decide what action you need to take to protect people's health.

The survey and the action list will form an asbestos management plan. A step by step guide to managing asbestos, including a sample asbestos management plan, is available free on the HSE website: www.hse.gov.uk/asbestos/managing. Most farmers should be able to complete the plan themselves. You may presume any suspect materials to be ACMs without further analysis.

Well-sealed, undamaged asbestos is often best left alone, but ACMs that are damaged may be better removed. If in doubt, ask for expert help. Work with asbestos insulation, asbestos board or sprayed coatings (ie limpet asbestos) must be carried out by specialist licensed contractors.

You must make sure that everyone, especially contractors, working on the farm buildings is made aware of the presence of asbestos and you must take appropriate steps to protect their health. Places where ACMs have been identified must be labelled. Inhaling asbestos fibres as a result of disturbing the fabric of a building can be fatal.

Demolition or dismantling

Like all construction work, this must be planned. Ensure you have made arrangements to bring the structure down in a way that prevents danger. Make sure you have enough time to demolish or dismantle the building. If any debris or parts of the structure are left standing because you do not have time to finish the job, they need to be left in a stable condition so they will not collapse.

Demolition of buildings containing ACMs is specialist work and should be carried out by licensed contractors. If intact asbestos cement sheets need to be disposed of, you will need to contact your local authority to find out details of your nearest licensed site and the bagging arrangements that are needed for safe disposal. Alternatively, a licensed waste contractor may dispose of them for you.

New buildings

When putting up a new farm building, consider:

- Does the location provide good access for farm vehicles?
- Is it likely you will want to change what the building is used for?
- How easy will it be to maintain?
- What are the locations of any overhead power lines?

It is easy to build safety problems into a building and just as easy to engineer out these problems at the start.

Find out more

Managing health and safety in construction L153
Managing asbestos in buildings: A brief guide INDG223(rev5)
Need building work done? A short guide for clients on the Construction (Design and Management) Regulations 2015 INDG411
Health and safety in roofwork HSG33

Further information about CDM2015 can be found at: www.hse.gov.uk/construction

10 Workplace transport

The most common causes of serious and fatal injuries in agriculture involve moving and overturning vehicles. Transport movements in and around the workplace need to be controlled to protect pedestrians and to prevent damage to equipment and buildings. Other incidents happen when people leave a vehicle without making sure it cannot move or cause injury in other ways. The vehicle braking system must be properly maintained and you should also lower to the ground any raised implements or loaders.

'Safe stop' is the most important safety action of all:

- handbrake on;
- controls in neutral;
- engine off and remove key.

Because of the wide variety of activities involving transport in agriculture, it is easier to identify problems and take action if you break your transport activities into three areas:

- vehicle;
- driver;
- site.

Safe vehicle

Check that vehicles, machines and handling equipment are:

- capable of safely performing the jobs to be done, with reversing aids such as mirrors;
- inspected daily and faults repaired promptly;
- properly maintained, paying particular attention to braking systems.

Check that your vehicles, or any machines with workers riding or working on them, are fitted with roll-over protective structures (ROPS) and seatbelts if there is a risk of overturning.

Check that:

- drivers of lift trucks and loaders are protected from falling objects;
- loads are stable and secure;
- trailers have adequate brakes designed for the maximum loads and speeds at which they will operate;
- keys are kept secure when vehicles are not in use.

Safe driver

Check that drivers:

- are medically fit to drive;
- are properly trained and unauthorised people are not allowed to drive;
- know how to safely enter and exit the vehicle.

Never allow passengers to ride on or in vehicle cabs unless they are sitting on a passenger seat in a safe position and cannot impede the driver, accidentally contact the machine controls, or obscure the driver's vision.

Safe site

Check that:

- vehicles and pedestrians are separated where possible;
- visiting drivers are aware of your rules, including parking areas, one-way systems etc;
- vehicle routes reduce the need to reverse, eg by adding turning circles, or using one-way systems;
- traffic routes are properly maintained and adequately lit;
- warning and speed limit signs are clear and consistent with the Highway Code.

Overturning tractors and other self-propelled vehicles

You may only use a tractor or machine without ROPS in low-risk situations such as buildings and orchards or where specific exemptions exist. Where roll-over protection is fitted, you should also have seatbelts fitted if a machine will be used in situations where there is a risk of overturning. To reduce the risk of an overturn:

- make sure that tractors and machines are properly equipped and maintained, especially brakes, steering and tyres. Consider wide wheel settings for work on slopes;
- plan the operation in advance, and make sure operators know the key elements of safe working on slopes.

Remember:

- You should always turn uphill when working across a slope, and descend straight down the gentlest gradient.
- You cannot always safely descend a slope that you safely drove up.
- Tractor rear-wheel grip lessens as the load of a rear-mounted machine is emptied.
- Tractors with trailed rollers, four-wheel trailers etc will have extra thrust imposed with no additional weight – they may slide away out of control.

To reduce the risk of injury if you do overturn:

- stay in the cab and do not attempt to jump clear, as most deaths and serious injuries involve those who jump or are thrown out of a cab during overturning;
- check that the safety frame or cab is in good condition and correctly fitted. Corrosion and incorrect mounting bolts can cause the safety frame to fail in an overturn;
- never remove windows or doors from a safety cab;
- wear the seatbelts fitted, as this is a legal requirement where there is a risk of overturning. Consider fitting belts where not installed as original equipment;
- don't carry loose items inside the cab as they may cause extra injury in an overturn.

All-terrain vehicles

ATVs such as quad bikes and side-by-side utility vehicles are designed to cope with a wide variety of off-road conditions, but if used carelessly can very rapidly become unstable. Many quad bike fatalities in the UK have been caused by head injuries. Helmets would have prevented most, if not all, of these deaths. You should always wear a helmet when riding a quad bike.

The long seat on a quad bike allows operators to shift their body weight backwards and forwards for different slope conditions, a technique known as 'active' riding. It is **not** for carrying passengers.

To help reduce the risks:

- carry out safety checks and maintenance in accordance with the manufacturer's recommendations, eg regularly check tyre pressures, brakes and throttle;
- secure loads on racks and make sure they are evenly balanced;
- always read and follow the owner's manual;
- stick to planned routes, where possible, and walk new routes if necessary to check for hidden obstructions, hollows or other hazards;
- take extra care with trailed or mounted equipment and understand how they affect stability;
- make sure all riders receive adequate training.

Never carry a child as a passenger; it is illegal and will reduce your ability to control the ATV. Children under 13 years old are prohibited from using an ATV at work. Over-13s should only ride ATVs – of an appropriate size and power – after formal training on a low-power ATV.

On the road

Specific legislation applies to vehicles which travel on public highways. The primary enforcement bodies are the police and VOSA (Vehicle and Operator Services Agency), who should be consulted for specific detailed advice.

Carrying dangerous goods

Under the Carriage of Dangerous Goods and Use of Transportable Pressure Equipment Regulations 2009, certain rules apply when you carry dangerous goods by road, eg acids, ammonium nitrate fertilisers, pesticides, diesel fuel etc. Exemptions exist for trailers towed by agricultural or forestry tractors but these do not apply for other vehicles such as Land Rovers. More details can be found at www.hse.gov.uk/cdg/manual/exemptions.htm.

Telescopic materials handlers (telehandlers)

As with all lifting equipment, work with telehandlers should be planned and the risks assessed to ensure the work can be carried out safely.

Most machines feature a side-mounted cab, with the boom mounted centrally or to the right of the machine chassis. The operator's view from the cab may be obstructed or 'masked' by the boom, cab pillars and other parts of the structure. Restricted visibility from the cab can also be a problem when reversing and when lifting large loads.

Telehandlers should only be driven by authorised, trained and competent people who have completed appropriate training and testing (see HSE Approved Code of Practice L117 in 'Find out more').

Hazards associated with telehandler operation can include:

■ overturning – during travel or when lifting, on slopes or flat ground;
■ electrocution – from contact with OHPLs;
■ unsecured loads falling from height, eg bales;
■ using inappropriate, unsecured or poorly maintained handling attachments;
■ unsafe procedures, eg using a grain bucket to knock in fence posts;
■ people falling from height, eg when using attachments as work platforms;
■ unintended movement of the machine.

Before using a telehandler you should make sure:

■ the machine is of a type suitable for the environment in which it is to be used and is capable of performing the required tasks safely;
■ attachments are suitable, compatible with the machine, and safe to use;
■ visibility aids such as mirrors are in good condition and properly adjusted, and the cab windows are clean. The glass for the window nearest the boom must always be intact to prevent the risk of crushing from the boom;
■ the machine is properly maintained in accordance with the manufacturer's recommendations;
■ the operator is familiar with the controls and has read and understood the operator's manual;
■ all recommended pre-use checks have been carried out, including a check that the overload indicator is in working order;
■ wherever possible, pedestrians are separated from telehandler operations.

When using a telehandler:

■ travel with the boom lowered to make sure that the centre of gravity of the machine and the load is as low as possible to maximise stability;
■ carefully choose routes to avoid OHPLs, very steep slopes or gradients and slippery or loose surfaces;
■ adopt the correct driving direction and travelling position for negotiating a slope or gradient, eg when a load is carried the load should face uphill. When no load is carried the fork arms should face downhill;
■ avoid turning on or traversing a slope or gradient and always descend straight down the gentlest gradient of a slope, instead of driving diagonally across it;
■ avoid stacking/de-stacking a load on a slope or gradient where you can;
■ use suitable scotches or supports if any work has to be carried out under a raised boom.

The operator should always look around and check for the presence of pedestrians before moving off and while manoeuvring and travelling.

Lifting operations

Properly plan and organise the lift, using appropriate equipment and competent people, to minimise the risks. Make sure:

■ all lifting equipment is thoroughly examined (and tested if necessary) regularly by a competent person. Independent inspection organisations, including insurance companies, can help;
■ safe working loads (SWLs) are marked on lifting equipment. Never exceed SWLs, or use damaged, makeshift or worn items;
■ never use grain buckets, pallets or other makeshift equipment for lifting people off the ground (see section 8 'Preventing falls').

Find out more

Rider-operated lift trucks: Operator training and safe use. Approved Code of Practice and guidance L117
Safe use of ATVs in agriculture and forestry AIS33(rev1)
Using tractors safely: A step-by-step guide INDG185(rev3)
Vehicle health check scheme: www.bagma.com

11 Selecting and using work equipment

Machinery

Many serious incidents on farms involve machinery, often during maintenance or unblocking. Some happen because a machine has been used for a job for which it is unsuitable; others because guards have not been provided or have been left off. PTO shafts have been involved in many fatal injuries, often with machines used while stationary, such as for slurry handling or feed milling and mixing.

Buying machinery can be one of the biggest investments you make, and the profitability of the business can depend on it doing the right job well, safely, and without affecting people's health.

When buying new machinery, check:

- it is 'CE' marked and supplied with a Certificate of Conformity. This is a legal requirement and represents the manufacturer's claim to have built the machine to meet legal safety requirements;

- it is suitable for the intended use, eg compatible with tractors, trailers have adequate braking systems for the maximum load and speed intended etc;
- for good driver visibility and ways this can be improved for safe reversing, eg by specifying CCTV, audible reversing warning devices, better mirrors;
- tractors and other self-propelled machines are fitted with suitable ROPS and falling object protection structures (FOPS) – see section 10 'Workplace transport');
- the maximum operating height of machines such as combines, telescopic handlers, sprayers and forage harvesters. Any 33 000- and 11 000-volt OHPLs on your land should be at least 5.2 m from the ground but, if you are in any doubt, contact the distribution network operator (DNO) to have them checked. Make sure machines you buy have sufficient clearance to pass safely under OHPLs;
- likely dust or fume emissions and take these into account where you have a choice of machines;
- for ease of maintenance. A machine which is designed to be easily and safely maintained will save you time and reduce risks;
- what steps the manufacturer has taken to make it safe for you to clear blockages. Machines prone to blockages, such as balers, should be designed to minimise them and have a suitable way of clearing them, eg a pick-up reversing mechanism;
- instructions are provided as well as a workshop manual if you intend to service the machine yourself. Make sure your operators read these instructions;
- information on noise and vibration levels is included in the operator's manual. You may need to provide extra operator protection yourself if the levels exceed the legal requirements (see section 22 'Noise and vibration');
- whether operators need training to use the machine safely. Ask the supplier to provide initial training/instruction and consider if your operator will need further formal training, eg for telescopic loaders, ATVs and chainsaws.

When buying second-hand machines, check:

- tractors and machinery comply with the requirements of PUWER. If not, they must be brought up to the required standard before being used;
- the operator's manual is provided or you can get hold of suitable information (eg from the original manufacturer, supplying dealer, or the internet);
- any missing or damaged guards can be replaced or repaired before using the machine.

When you buy or hire machines the law requires the supplier to provide necessary safeguards.

Using machines safely

- Make sure the machine is suitable for the job (eg a bale spike used to lift anything other than bales, or a telescopic handler with a grain bucket used to lift a person for work at a height, would not be suitable).
- You should be able to recognise dangerous parts and think about how to prevent injury when carrying out your risk assessment.

- When you decide on controls, consider not only your disciplined and trained workers but also those who are tired, distracted or less experienced.
- If you provide safeguards which are inconvenient to use, or which can be too easily removed, you may inadvertently encourage your employees to take risks, suffer injury and break the law.
- You should have a system to check that work equipment, including machinery, is safe to use. Tell people if it is not working properly.
- If safety depends on how the equipment has been installed, inspect it to ensure it has been set up correctly and is safe to operate before you use it for the first time, and after assembly in a new location.
- Inspect equipment regularly for deterioration which might result in danger (such as corrosion on roll frames), and whenever there have been exceptional circumstances that may make the equipment unsafe. Keep records of all inspections.

Make sure you and your workers:

- use machines according to the instructions supplied with them;
- know how to stop the machine safely before operating it;
- understand how to carry out the 'safe stop' procedure;
- know how to clear blockages safely, using the reversing mechanism or tools provided with the machine;
- always start machines from the correct position;
- check all guards are fitted and working correctly;
- maintain machines so they can be used safely;
- 'safety check' all equipment and put right all defects before each use;
- check that controls are clearly marked to show what they do, which machine they control and are designed and placed so you cannot operate them accidentally;
- check the area around fixed machines is clean, tidy and free from obstruction;
- check that fixed or stationary machines are adequately lit;
- check that electrical machinery is isolated and locked-off if safeguards are removed;
- are trained to work safely;
- are provided with and use necessary protective clothing.

Never:

- use a machine unless you know how to use it safely and have received suitable training;
- attempt to clear blockages or clean a machine unless you have followed the 'safe stop' procedure, the drive is disconnected, the machine is stationary and components have stopped;
- wear long chains, loose clothing, gloves or rings, or keep long hair loose, which may get caught up in moving parts;
- distract people who are using machines;
- dismount from a moving tractor or other self-propelled machine.

Power take-off shaft guards

For PTO shaft guards, check that the guard is:

- made to a recognised standard such as BS EN ISO 5674;
- the correct size and length for the shaft, both when closed and when extended;
- a non-rotating type, with the restraining device, eg securing chains, in place;
- properly used and maintained. Clean and lubricate guards regularly;
- supported when not connected. Do not rest it on the drawbar or drop it on the ground, and do not suspend it by the restraining device;
- safe from damage, eg from contact with the lower link arms on the tractor or when the machine is parked and not in use.

Make sure no one uses adaptors to allow a six-spline shaft to drive 1000 rpm machines.

Other dangerous parts

Check that safeguards are fitted, and make sure they are:

- strong enough and securely attached to the machine;
- not easily defeated, eg require a tool to open, and are self-locking;
- made of suitable material. Plastic allows good visibility but may be easily damaged;
- regularly checked and maintained in effective working order.

If guards are interlocked, eg if you need access several times each day to a dangerous part, check that:

- the machine cannot start before the guard is in position;
- opening the guard stops the machine or that part;
- the interlocking switch or valve is sufficiently robust for the job, and the way it works makes it difficult for someone to defeat.

Find out more

Power take-offs and power take-off drive shafts AIS40
Working safely with agricultural machinery INDG241(rev1)
Buying new machinery INDG271(rev1)

12 Maintenance work

All equipment and plant should be maintained in good working order and in good repair, and some must be regularly checked. In maintenance work, conditions are very different from those normally encountered and new hazards may be introduced. It is essential that everyone involved is trained to be aware of the hazards and the correct precautions.

Plant and equipment

Some equipment should be regularly examined or tested by a competent person, eg lifting equipment such as chains and ropes, steam boilers, or air receivers such as those on compressors. Consult an independent inspection organisation or your insurance company for advice.

Follow the manufacturer's recommended maintenance schedules for work equipment such as tractors and vehicles, lift trucks, ATVs (quad bikes), portable electrical equipment, and farm machinery.

Maintenance

When you are carrying out maintenance operations follow the 'safe stop' procedure and make sure:

- all movement has stopped before removing any guards;
- workers are properly trained to do the job;
- adequate tools and instructions are provided for maintaining, adjusting, cleaning and unblocking machines;
- safe working practices are devised and used;
- stored energy, eg from compressed material, springs or hydraulics, is released safely before you start work;
- hydraulically-raised machines or parts are prevented from descending by using mechanical devices such as stops or jacks when people work under them.

Vehicle repair

During vehicle repair:

- make sure brakes are applied and wheels chocked;
- always prop raised bodies and do not rely on hydraulic systems for support;
- start and run engines with brakes on and in neutral gear;
- never work under vehicles supported on jacks alone – always use axle stands;
- beware of the explosion risk when draining and repairing fuel tanks. Use a retriever/adaptor to drain petrol from tanks and lines in a safe place away from drains, pits, openings in the ground and sources of ignition;
- avoid burns from battery short circuits by disconnecting the battery before starting work;
- older brake linings may also contain asbestos. Never 'blow out' brakes, always use a vacuum or other dust-free method. Do not use asbestos brake lining as a replacement.

Isolating equipment

Isolate machines before any maintenance, cleaning or adjustment. It is not enough just to switch the machine off – you need to use the main isolator, usually a separate control. If the machine is at some distance from the isolator, or if work in progress is not obvious, remove the fuses from the isolator box and attach a 'danger' tag to it, or lock the isolator box and keep the key safe.

General workshop safety

Check that:

- you keep the workshop tidy and avoid tripping hazards such as trailing cables, tools etc;
- welding gas bottles are secured upright, and when in use can be moved easily on a trolley;
- battery charging is done in a well-ventilated area away from sources of ignition such as welding flames or angle grinding;
- you avoid chlorinated solvents such as 'trike' or 'perc' for degreasing. Use a less harmful product (not paraffin or petrol) and put degreasing baths in well-ventilated areas;

- arc welding is done in a protected area so that others nearby are not affected by the ultra-violet light and suffer 'arc-eye' as a result;
- you use the correct abrasive wheel for the job and adjust bench grinder tool-rests close to the wheel;
- you can escape from inspection pits easily and that inspection lamps have protected bulbs (flammable fluids such as petrol may collect in the bottom of the pit and explode with the heat from a broken bulb filament);
- noise levels from plant such as compressors are controlled – site the machine in a separate closed area or outside;
- hand tools are in good condition and suitable for the job;
- PPE is provided – eye protection for chiselling, grinding and welding work; respiratory protection for work that creates dust, if extraction cannot be provided; or foot protection if there is a risk of things falling onto the feet.

Pressurised plant

Any plant or equipment under pressure, such as slurry tankers, boilers and air receivers, may burst violently. Reduce the chances of this happening and anyone being killed or injured. Make sure:

- the plant is suitable for its intended purpose and installed correctly;
- you know the safe working pressure and temperatures of any pressurised system or equipment;
- safety valves are fitted to relieve excess pressure, as well as safety devices to make over- or under-pressurisation unlikely, such as boiler low water level alarms;
- you avoid accidentally pressurising any system or equipment, eg provide boiler 'blowdown' tanks with an adequately sized vent pipe. Applying heat to drums or tanks which have contained flammable material may create pressure, so always cold-cut sealed containers.

Wheel changing

Serious accidents, including fatalities, have been caused by unsafe practices during wheel/tyre changing and when inflating tyres. When using jacks to lift or support vehicles or machines:

- use the correct jack for the job, capable of supporting the load imposed on it;
- use the correct jacking point, as identified on the machine or in the operator's manual;
- position axle stands to give additional support;
- chock the other wheels to prevent movement;
- carry out the work on firm, level ground.

Tyre/wheel repair and replacement should only be tackled by competent staff. Take extra care with split-rim wheels as these present additional hazards. Although they are becoming less common, you may find them on older vehicles such as forklift trucks, loading shovels and former military vehicles. If in doubt seek help from a specialist.

Don't use 'unrestricted' airlines (without a gauge or pressure control device) or valve connectors that require the operator to hold them in place when inflating tyres. Tyres can explode if they are not inflated safely. Use airline hoses long enough to allow the operator to stay outside the likely explosion path during inflation. Wheel cages and similar devices can help reduce the risk of injury. For safety advice on wheels and tyres – see 'Find out more'.

The average size of wheels and tyres has increased significantly, which creates a greater risk of manual handling injuries because they are heavier and more difficult to hold and manoeuvre. Changing large tractor wheels can be made easier with an appropriate mechanical handling trolley.

Repairs in the field

Recovering or repairing vehicles and machines in the field can introduce new hazards and create additional risks. In some circumstances, it may be safer to attempt the repair in the workshop rather than in the field. Where you have to carry out repairs or maintenance in the field, eg where a machine has broken down, it is important to ensure you assess all risks properly before tackling the job. Factors to consider may include:

- the impact of adverse weather conditions such as wind or rain;
- poor lighting, eg at dusk;
- ground conditions, eg wet or soft surfaces;
- the location of OHPLs;
- the need to ensure safety for access or work at height, eg on combines.

Always plan the job and use safe systems of work whether in the workshop or in the field.

Find out more

Working safely with agricultural machinery INDG241(rev1)
Pressure systems: A brief guide to safety INDG261(rev2)
Health and safety in motor vehicle repair and associated industries HSG261

13 Workplace safety and welfare

Many of the specific risks on your farm will have been covered

The law

The Workplace (Health, Safety and Welfare) Regulations 1992 aim to protect the health and safety of everyone in the workplace, and to make sure that adequate welfare facilities are provided for people at work. The Confined Spaces Regulations 1997 set out precautions that must be taken before work in a confined space. The Health and Safety (Safety Signs and Signals) Regulations 1996 require a safety sign where there is significant risk to health and safety not controlled by other methods.

in other sections of *Farmwise*. You also need to look at the activities that take place in your workplace as a whole:

- Slips, trips and falls can happen anywhere in workplaces, such as in buildings or yards. Keep floor surfaces level where you can, eg by filling in holes.
- Make sure no one can fall from open edges such as catwalks above grain bins or feed lofts. You must also take action if there is a risk of injury from falls into tanks, pits or onto projecting objects. Fixed guardrails or fencing at least 950 mm above the working surface will be suitable.
- Check working areas are free from obstructions, such as trailing cables, sacks or pallets, and there is enough space for storing tools and materials.
- Keep your buildings in good repair, making sure floors are not overloaded, especially in feed lofts or older buildings. Management of asbestos-containing material is covered in section 9 'Building work'.
- Remember, visiting workers such as lorry drivers, agronomists and vets are also at risk and you have a duty to make sure they are safe when they are on your premises or farm.

Provide:

- handrails on stairs and ramps where necessary, and safety hoops or rest stages on long vertical fixed ladders used regularly, eg for external access to grain bins;
- good drainage in wet processes such as vegetable washing areas or dairies, and keep outdoor routes clear, eg salted, sanded or swept during icy conditions;
- adequate and suitable lighting. Use natural light where possible, but try to avoid glare. Note that some fluorescent tubes flicker and can be dangerous, making rotating machinery appear stationary. Moving from light to dark and vice versa increases the risk of slips and trips. Well-lit outside areas will help security;
- adequate temperature and ventilation, including fresh air when working inside;
- safety signs where a significant risk to health and safety

remains after you have taken other control measures identified by your risk assessment.

Workplaces can cause health problems, so make sure you provide:

- seats with a backrest supporting the small of the back and, if needed, a footrest, where work can be done seated, eg vegetable grading;
- machine controls designed and arranged to provide a comfortable working position;
- engineering controls, eg local exhaust ventilation (LEV) systems, to reduce health risks from dangerous substances such as grain dust;
- well-designed tools and working areas to reduce hand and forearm injury caused by repetitive movements, eg on vegetable or fruit grading lines.

Toilet and welfare facilities

There is a risk of illness from hazardous substances and from muck or other animal products carrying potentially hazardous micro-organisms. If you have full- or part-time, casual or permanent workers, provide rest facilities and:

- clean, well-ventilated toilets;
- wash basins with hot and cold (or warm) running water, soap and towels (or a hand dryer);
- portable toilet and washing facilities for workers working away from base;
- changing facilities where special clothing is worn;
- a clean drinking water supply (marked to distinguish it from any non-drinkable supply).

Confined spaces

There have been deaths in confined spaces on farms. Sometimes more than one person has been killed – the second person often being a would-be rescuer.

A confined space is anywhere that, because it is enclosed, gives rise to a risk of serious injury from fire or explosion, loss of consciousness from lack of oxygen, drowning, or asphyxiation due to being trapped by a free-flowing solid. Confined spaces on farms are found in:

■ produce stores such as grain/forage silos and bins, or controlled atmosphere fruit and vegetable stores;
■ pits such as grain elevator pits, slurry pits and chambers or vehicle inspection pits.

If you have areas which present any of these risks you must:

■ avoid working in the confined space if you can. Can the work be done from outside?
■ follow a safe system of work if you really have to work in a confined space. Consider:
  - the need for competent people;
  - testing the atmosphere to make sure it can support life, and does not contain dangerous levels of gases such as hydrogen sulphide. Remember that some areas such as slurry pits may continue to give off poisonous gases after testing;
  - whether the area is adequately ventilated before entry;
  - providing PPE, including breathing apparatus;
■ make arrangements in case something goes wrong. Never enter the confined space without making proper emergency arrangements. Rescue equipment, including harnesses and safety lines, should be provided. Ensure you can rapidly notify the emergency services if necessary.

Forage tower and sealed moist grain silos are confined spaces. They should not be entered without appropriate safety precautions because of the danger of high concentrations of toxic gases and oxygen depletion. Anyone entering must follow the procedures for working in confined spaces shown above.

Spaces with limited ventilation

Gases can also build up to dangerous levels in areas that have restricted ventilation. Slurry gases can be present in slatted cattle housing or poorly ventilated areas as well as confined spaces. Hydrogen sulphide is highly toxic, heavier than air and odourless at high concentrations.

■ Consider where gases may build up and not be dispersed by draughts and breezes, eg if your reception pit is in a depression in the ground, or positioned between buildings.
■ Put up signs warning gases may be present and make sure everyone on the farm knows to avoid these areas during operations such as slurry agitation.

Nitrogen dioxide and carbon dioxide can be present in silage clamps, particularly under the sheeting – nitrogen dioxide can cause permanent damage to your throat and lungs and can kill. Nitrogen dioxide is heavier than air and can collect around the edges and walls of the silage clamp. Good ventilation will disperse these gases but gases trapped under the sheeting will still be present.

■ Never crawl under silage clamp sheeting.
■ Make sure children do not play in this area.

■ Avoid the risk of gases being generated by careful clamp consolidation and completed, well-sealed clamp sheeting.

Fire precautions in workplaces

Assess the risks from fire and make sure:

■ you have safe means of escape, kept free from obstructions and clearly marked;
■ everyone knows what to do if a fire starts, especially how to raise the alarm. Display fire action instructions and have a fire drill periodically;
■ any fire alarms work (check them weekly) and that they can be heard everywhere over normal background noise;
■ you have enough extinguishers, of the right type and properly maintained, to deal promptly with small outbreaks of fire. Make sure workers know how to use them.

Fertiliser storage

Store all fertilisers safely. Special requirements apply for the storage of ammonium nitrate (AN) fertiliser. It can help other materials to burn and in certain circumstances it can explode and give off toxic fumes.

■ Storage buildings should be constructed of non-combustible material and should not contain other combustible materials.
■ Where this is not reasonably practicable, store AN fertilisers as far away as possible from combustible materials and never within 2 m.
■ If you are storing 150 tonnes or more of AN, and the nitrogen content exceeds 15.75% by weight, you must notify your local Fire & Rescue Service.

Consider the specific risks on your farm

■ Do you use mobile gas heaters, eg in caravans or for gas brooders? Are they maintained and placed in areas with adequate ventilation for workers?
■ Have you introduced new risks, eg biodiesel production? Where are you making it and where are you storing it?
■ Are you diversifying, eg with open farms and shops? Have you assessed the risks of access by the general public and any vehicle movement risks and traffic organisation problems?
■ Is there a level crossing on your farm or on land where you work? You need to make sure that both you and others using it on your behalf are aware of what they need to do to use the crossing safely.

Find out more

Guidance on storing pesticides for farmers and other professional users AIS16(rev1)
Confined spaces: A brief guide to working safely INDG258(rev1)
Storing and handling ammonium nitrate INDG230
The Dangerous Substances (Notification and Marking of Sites) Regulations 1990 (NAMOS): A brief guide on an amendment to the Regulations 2013 INDG467
Workplace health, safety and welfare: A short guide for managers INDG244(rev2)

14 Electricity

People are killed or seriously injured by electricity in agriculture every year, but there are many more incidents that damage equipment and thousands of 'near-misses', any of which could have had fatal consequences. Many of these involve contact with OHPLs and cause disruption and costs to farmers, other businesses and the community. Others involve poorly maintained hand-held equipment or extension cables. Poor electrical installations and equipment can also cause fires, resulting in significant losses in buildings, equipment and livestock.

Overhead power lines

Electricity can jump gaps when equipment or machinery gets close enough – you do not need to contact OHPLs for electricity to be conducted through it to earth. Anyone touching the machinery at the same time will receive an electric shock. If OHPLs run across your land, consider with your distribution network operator whether they can be re-routed, put underground, or raised. If that cannot be done, make sure you have a map of the routes of the lines (available from your DNO) and that visiting workers such as contractors have copies (include details of OHPLs in contracts).

Where possible, do not carry out the following operations within a horizontal distance of at least 10 m from OHPLs:

- stacking bales or potato boxes;
- erecting temporary structures such as polytunnels;
- jobs involving moving ladders or irrigation pipes;
- folding sprayer booms;
- tipping trailers or lorries;
- operating lift trucks or telescopic handlers;
- working with or on top of combines or other high machinery;
- tree work.

If you cannot avoid carrying out any of these activities closer than 10 m, consult your DNO for advice. If the line cannot be moved or made dead you will need to assess the risks and agree a safe system of work.

Reduce risks by:

- planning and marking safe routes and designate safe areas for high-risk operations, eg for using telescopic handlers and tipping trailers at storage or loading areas;
- checking the maximum operating height of machines such as combines, telescopic handlers, sprayers and forage harvesters. Any 33 000- and 11 000-volt OHPLs on your land should be at least 5.2 m from the ground but, if you are in any doubt, contact the DNO to have them checked. Ensure enough clearance under power lines;
- fitting shorter radio aerials or repositioning existing ones on high machines so they cannot cause danger;
- using sprayers with horizontally folding booms and never folding them on the move;
- taking care not to damage poles and stays;
- carrying irrigation pipes horizontally, using two people and not storing pipes or other materials and equipment near or under power lines and their supports;
- not erecting fencing wire under or adjacent to OHPLs, nor moving or straining fencing wire where it may spring up and come into contact with the line. Long runs of wire on undulating ground present a special risk;
- knowing what to do in an emergency – obtain contact details of relevant DNOs, display this information in the cabs of machines and store the number in your mobile phone.

If you have to work near OHPLs, check with your DNO and, if necessary, arrange temporary disconnection.

What if you come into contact with an OHPL?

- If part of a vehicle or load is in contact with an OHPL, the operator should remain in the cab and call the DNO on 105 immediately.
- Keep others away.
- Try to drive clear. If this is not possible, **jump well clear** so that no simultaneous contact is made between you, the vehicle and the ground.
- Never attempt to disentangle equipment until the owner of the line has confirmed that it has been de-energised and made safe.
- **Warning**: Contact with an OHPL may cause the power supply to 'trip out' temporarily and it may be reconnected and re-energised automatically, without warning.
- Do not return to a machine for any reason unless you have received confirmation that it is safe to do so.

What can happen if you come into contact with an OHPL

Underground cables

If you suspect there are underground cables owned by the DNO in the vicinity of where you propose to excavate, ask the DNO and landowner for plans to confirm their location. If they are in close proximity to the working area you may need to ask someone from the DNO to come and accurately locate them for you. If you are excavating where your own cables are present, then someone who is experienced in underground cable detection techniques should help you locate them.

Your electrical system

Make sure:

- there is an accessible and clearly identified switch near each fixed machine to cut off power in an emergency;
- power cables to machines are suitably protected (armoured cable, covered in thick flexible rubber or neoprene, or installed in conduit) with a good earth connection;
- light bulbs are protected, eg use bulkhead-type fittings;
- you avoid using extension leads by ensuring there are enough socket outlets – overloading sockets by using adaptors is a fire hazard. In suitable places, eg the farm office, you can use a multi-plug socket block;
- three-pin plugs always have the flex firmly clamped to stop the wires, particularly the earth, pulling out of the terminals;
- fuses, circuit breakers etc are correctly rated for the circuit they protect. Fuses must never be bypassed, over-wired or wrapped with foil;
- you have an appropriate plug and socket suitable for the environment where it is to be used (eg to BS EN 60309–1) and for equipment drawing a heavy current, eg welders;
- outdoor socket outlets, that are located in damp or corrosive atmospheres, or where steam or water jets are used, are of an appropriate type and protected by a residual current device (RCD). Get advice – never use a household-type socket;
- covers to electrical equipment are kept closed and, if possible, locked, with the key held by a responsible person;
- main switches are readily accessible and clearly identified, everyone knows how to use them in an emergency, and how to securely isolate circuits;
- wiring is installed in protective conduit or similar to avoid damage by rats and mice;
- installations are checked periodically and repairs carried out by a competent electrician;
- damaged cables are isolated and repaired or replaced immediately.

Portable equipment

Electrical tools used outdoors or where there is a lot of earthed metalwork should be operated at reduced voltage from a safety isolating transformer (eg 110 volts centre tapped to earth) or be connected through an RCD which will cut off the power quickly if there is an earth fault. Consider whether you can avoid using electricity altogether, eg by using pneumatic tools in the workshop, but check the noise levels are not too high.

Make sure you and your workers:

- use electrical plugs and fittings that are sufficiently robust and suitable for the wet or dusty conditions likely to be found in agriculture;
- regularly inspect the wiring and condition of all portable tools. Don't forget hired or borrowed tools;
- take suspect or faulty tools out of use, put them in a secure place and make sure they are not used until repaired by a competent person;
- make someone responsible for regularly operating the 'test' button on RCDs to ensure they work correctly;
- switch off tools and power sockets before plugging in;
- unplug or isolate appliances before cleaning or making adjustments;
- provide sufficient socket outlets to keep the use of extension leads to a minimum. When an extension lead has to be used, check it is in good condition and that it is positioned where it won't be damaged or create a tripping hazard;
- on welding sets, only use insulated leads and undamaged electrode holders.

Electric shock

It is important to know what to do if someone receives an electric shock. Remember always to disconnect the power source first. If that is not possible, never touch the electrocuted person except with non-conducting items and never use metal. Resuscitation needs training and practice so make sure you and your workers receive elementary first-aid training. You can also display an 'electric shock poster', which shows what to do (see 'Find out more').

Find out more

Working safely near overhead electricity power lines AIS8(rev3)
Avoiding danger from overhead power lines GS6
Maintaining portable and transportable electrical equipment HSG107
Electric shock: First aid procedures (poster)
Further information is available from your local DNO and the Energy Networks Association: www.energynetworks.org

15 Child and public safety

Every year children are killed during agricultural work activities. People often believe that farm children understand farm risks, but the vast majority of children who die in farm incidents are family members. A few straightforward steps, and proper supervision of children, will reduce these risks.

Other members of the public may also be at risk, eg when using public rights of way through fields containing cattle and calves.

The risks from machinery

The law says that no child under 13 may drive or ride on tractors and other self-propelled machines used in agriculture.

Before allowing children over 13 to operate a tractor, certain conditions must be met. These are described in full in HSE's free leaflet INDG472 *Preventing accidents to children on farms*.

Children under 16 must not drive, operate, or help to operate, any of the following:

- towed or self-propelled harvesters and processing machines;
- trailers or feed equipment with conveying, loading/ unloading or spreading mechanisms;
- power-driven machines with cutting, splitting, or crushing mechanisms or power-operated soil-engaging parts;
- chemical applicators such as mounted, trailed or knapsack sprayers;
- handling equipment such as lift trucks, skid steer loaders or certain ATVs.

It is illegal to carry children under 13 in the cab of an agricultural vehicle, and it is unsafe. Children can and do:

- fall from the doorway or the rear window;
- interfere with the operator's control of the vehicle;
- distract the operator or unintentionally operate controls, eg the parking brake or hydraulics, when the operator leaves the cab, eg to open a gate.

If you carry children or adults on trailers (eg for farm visits, or 'pick-your-own') make sure that:

- the trailer is in good condition, with all safety devices working;
- seating is provided and secured to the trailer. Well-made bales, if properly secured, may be adequate;
- guardrails are fitted around the trailer edges;
- there are safe mounting/dismounting arrangements;
- children are supervised by a responsible adult and there is a means of contacting the driver from the trailer.

If you have to leave machinery in an area accessed by members of the public, make sure it is left in a safe condition, with the keys removed, the cab locked, the controls in neutral, foreloaders etc lowered to the ground, and the parking brake applied or wheels chocked.

Make sure that contractors and visiting drivers have clearly defined directions on where to park, load and unload and where to wait. This is particularly important if you are aware of public access routes across yards or if the delivery zone is adjacent to the farmhouse.

The risks from animals

Animals do not need to attack to pose a danger to people:

- A 'playful' bull, cow, sheep or pig can kill or severely injure.
- Veterinary medicines and application equipment can cause ill health.
- Diseases can be passed from animals to humans.

Check that children or other members of the public:

- cannot enter any yard or pen etc occupied by potentially dangerous animals. Remember that female animals, especially those with young, can kill or injure anyone, including children;
- do not have access to or use any form of chemicals or veterinary medicines and products, eg hypodermic syringes. Lock them away;
- do not look after animals or poultry without competent supervision.

Normally, you will not be required to provide PPE to children or members of the public visiting your farm. If PPE is required for young workers this should be appropriate to the task, eg a suitable riding hat.

Remember, if you have fields with rights of way or other permitted public access, make sure:

■ you do not keep bulls of recognised dairy breeds in fields with footpaths;

■ you assess the temperament of **any** cattle kept in fields with public access, and remove from the group any with a history of aggression, or that may be aggressive because of illness, young calves etc;

■ if you keep beef stock bulls in such fields, that they are accompanied by female stock and you put up suitable signs;

■ you consider whether it is reasonably practicable to temporarily fence rights of way so that cattle cannot access them.

The risks in the workplace

Farms are not playgrounds. Remember that children are naturally curious, and will often get into apparently inaccessible places. Make sure they are excluded from potentially dangerous areas, such as:

■ chemical stores;

■ slurry pits and lagoons (which may falsely appear safe to walk on);

■ reservoirs or sheep dips (which are often isolated);

■ grain intake pits and grain bins;

■ machinery or building maintenance activities.

To deter access to these areas use:

■ fencing, such as pig netting topped with two strands of barbed wire, to an overall height of at least 1.3 m. Gates should be sheeted, or otherwise impossible to climb, and padlocked;

■ grids (with a maximum aperture space of 62 mm); or

■ solid covers which will not move or give way if children stray onto them.

Also keep children away from yards or places with vehicle movements and make sure they are returned to a responsible adult if they stray into transport areas. Make sure everyone working on the farm is aware that children may be present. Explain that they are authorised to stop work if any children are in the work area and to send them somewhere safe.

Keep tools and work equipment secured.

Gates and wheels
Children may be tempted to climb on gates or wheels. Check that gates are properly erected and will not topple. Store flat or firmly secure upright any tractor wheels or gates not in use.

Stacks of hay or straw
Stacks of hay or straw appear ideal for making dens in, but they can collapse or catch fire, killing those under or on top of them. Check ladders have been stored safely where children cannot get at them, there is no evidence of children burrowing under stacks, and matches etc are kept in a safe place.

Grain bins
Grain bins also seem inviting places in which to play, until the grain begins to flow out and the child is drawn into the grain and drowns. Make sure children cannot gain access to bins, and check they are not in the store before starting machinery.

The risks on open farms and other visitor attractions

There are a number of diseases which people can catch from animals, eg through contact with faeces. The elderly and children are often particularly at risk from such diseases, which include infections from organisms such as cryptosporidium, campylobacter, E.coli O26 and O157 and salmonella. These infections can kill. If you invite the public onto your farm:

■ decide whether you want to allow visitors to have direct contact with the animals. Tell them about the risks and where and when they will be able to use washing facilities (in particular, remind nail biters, pen chewers and thumb suckers). Provide information signs to remind them;

■ washing facilities should be sufficient for the expected numbers of visitors needing to use them at one time, and should include running water (preferably warm), soap and paper towels;

■ alcohol gels and wipes are not a substitute for hand washing on farms;

■ provide training and supervision for workers on the need for visitors to wash and dry their hands thoroughly;

■ if you are selling food for human consumption do so only after visitors have passed animal contact areas and washing facilities;

■ do not allow eating in parts of the farm where animals can be touched.

The 'Industry Code of Practice' has more details on protecting visitors from diseases. See 'Find out more'.

If you open your farm to the public and schools on a regular basis you may wish to consider undertaking an accreditation course such as the Countryside Educational Visits Accreditation Scheme (CEVAS). Visit www.face-online.org.uk for more information.

Find out more

Preventing accidents to children on farms INDG472
Managing slurry on farms AIS9(rev2)
Cattle and public access in England and Wales AIS17EW(rev1)
Cattle and public access in Scotland AIS17S(rev1)
Industry Code of Practice: www.face-online.org.uk/codeofpractice

16 Handling livestock

Handling livestock always involves a risk of injury, so this advice will help you improve your handling system and make it safer and more efficient. Health hazards associated with livestock are covered in section 15 'Child and public safety', section 19 'Health problems in agriculture' and section 22 'Noise and vibration'.

What are the risks?

There is always a risk from crushing, kicking, butting or goring. The risk is greater if the animals have not been handled frequently, such as those from hills or moorland, sucklers or newly calved cows. Certain jobs may increase the risk, eg veterinary work.

Attempting to carry out stock tasks on unrestrained cattle or with makeshift equipment is particularly hazardous. Never underestimate the risk from cattle, even with good precautions in place.

Reduce the risks

To reduce the risk of injury to you and your employees, as well as visitors such as vets and statutory inspectors, when handling cattle you should have:

- proper handling facilities, which are well maintained and in good working order;
- a race and a crush suitable for the animals to be handled;
- trained and competent workers;
- a rigorous culling policy for temperamental animals.

The race

- Animals should be able to readily enter the race, which should have a funnel end.
- Make sure there is enough room in the collecting pen for them to feed into the funnel easily.
- A circular collecting pen means workers can stand safely behind a forcing gate as they move animals into the race, and keep the animals moving.
- Animals need to see clearly to the crush and beyond, so that they will readily move along the race.
- The race may be curved, but should not include tight turns.
- Animals are more prepared to move towards a light area than into the dark.

- The sides of the race should be high enough to prevent animals from jumping over them, and they should be properly secured to the ground and to each other for maximum strength.
- Sheet the sides of the race to help keep cattle moving by reducing distractions such as shadows and other animals.
- Contain the lead animal in the race while it waits its turn to enter the crush.
- Hinged or sliding doors are suitable, but be sure they are operated from the working side of the race so the operator does not have to reach across the race to close the gate.
- Never work on an animal in the crush with an unsecured animal waiting in the race behind.

The crush

A crush should allow most straightforward tasks to be carried out in safety (including oral treatments, ear tagging and work from the rear end). It should:

- have a locking front gate and yoke (ideally self-locking) to allow the animal's head to be firmly held. Additional head restraint will prevent the animal tossing its head up and injuring people;
- have a rump rail, chain or bar to minimise forward and backward movement of the animal. Always use this;
- be secured to the ground or, if mobile, to a vehicle;
- be positioned to allow you to work safely around it,

without the risk of contact with other animals, and have good natural or artificial lighting;

- allow gates etc to open smoothly with the minimum of effort and noise. Regular maintenance will help;
- have a slip-resistant floor, made of sound hardwood bolted into place (nails are not suitable), metal chequerplate, or with a rubber mat over the base.

Specialised tasks, such as belly or foot trimming, require a purpose-designed crush with adequate restraint and enough room to work safely.

Other equipment

- Consider the need for shedding gates after the crush to allow animals to be sorted into groups.
- Work around the crush will be more convenient if it is under cover with a workbench nearby (for documentation, veterinary medicines, instruments etc).
- Do not use makeshift gates and hurdles – they will make handling more difficult and increase the risk of injury.
- Never use sticks and prods to strike an animal – this may breach welfare legislation as well as agitating the animal.
- Before beginning work on any animal, check that it will be adequately restrained from kicking. Consider whether you should use an anti-kicking device.

For advice on keeping cattle in fields with public access, see section 15 'Child and public safety'.

Keeping bulls

Accidents, some of them fatal, happen every year because bulls are not treated with respect. Remember, a bull can kill you when he is being playful just as easily as when he is angry. Make sure you can handle your bull safely:

- Train bulls to associate people with feeding, grooming or exercise.
- Ring bulls at ten months old and inspect the ring regularly.
- Find out how bulls new to the farm have been handled, the equipment they are used to, and take time to get to know them.
- Check handlers are competent (with training and supervision as necessary), fit, knowledgeable about safety equipment to be used and aware of the dangers.
- Use handling aids such as bull poles and halters.
- Avoid running stock bulls through the milking parlour – separate them from cows using safe practices.
- Provide a purpose-built pen for dairy bulls. Make sure it has:
  - a lying and an exercise area;
  - outer walls at least 1.5 m high, strong enough to contain the bull;
  - facilities to allow feeding and watering from outside the pen;
  - fences, walls and gates which will not allow children or dogs through;
  - a remotely operated gate or yoke system which allows the bull to be restrained before anyone enters the pen;
  - a refuge or child-resistant emergency escape route.

No one should ever enter the enclosure when the bull is loose.

Preparing cattle for the abattoir

The Food Standards Agency (FSA) has produced advice on the husbandry systems farmers can adopt to keep cattle clean: *Clean beef cattle for slaughter: A guide for producers* (FSA/0951/1104) is available from their website at www.food.gov.uk/multimedia/pdfs/cleanbeefsaf1007.pdf. Putting these systems in place will reduce the need to clean cattle before they leave the farm.

Other livestock

Sheep – Reduce the risk of injury from handling smaller animals such as sheep by using races, shedding gates and turnover crates.

Pigs – Make full use of pig boards when moving or working among animals. Ensure the sow is properly restrained or segregated when working with piglets, especially in outdoor farrowing systems.

Find out more

Handling and housing cattle AIS35(rev1)

17 Chainsaws and tree work

The law

As well as the Provision and Use of Work Equipment Regulations 1998 (see section 11 'Selecting and using work equipment'), the Personal Protective Equipment at Work Regulations 1992 apply. Where risks to health and safety cannot be adequately controlled by other means, suitable PPE must be provided.

Work off the ground involving the lifting and lowering of people or loads, including work-positioning techniques, will be subject to the requirements of the Work at Height Regulations 2005 (WAHR) and the Lifting Operations and Lifting Equipment Regulations 1998 (LOLER).

Most farms have a chainsaw, which may be used for everything from cutting firewood and topping fence posts, to thinning coppices and felling large hardwoods. Some farms have forestry operations and use more complex machinery. All work with trees is high risk and safe systems of work must be provided.

No forestry machinery, particularly the farm chainsaw, should be used without adequate training, an understanding of the risks involved, the correct protective clothing and proper communication arrangements.

All workers who use a chainsaw should be competent to do so. Before using a chainsaw to carry out work on or in a tree, a worker should have received appropriate training and obtained a relevant certificate of competence or national competence award, unless they are undergoing such training and are adequately supervised.

This means everyone working with chainsaws on or in trees should hold such a certificate or award **unless**:

- it is being done as part of agricultural operations (eg hedging, clearing fallen branches, pruning trees to maintain clearance for machines); and
- the work is being done by the occupier or their employees; and
- they have used a chainsaw before 5 December 1998.

Everyone who uses a chainsaw at work for whatever task must have received adequate training.

Location

Check that:

- any overhead electric lines are further than two tree lengths from any tree to be felled or at least 10 m from any other tree work;
- you have agreed with your local DNO when the power is to be turned off;
- you have agreed with your local DNO when the power is to be re-energised;
- you have taken into account the position of roads, footpaths, or public access, and provided warning signs or barriers, or closed roads if necessary;
- you know the direction the tree will fall, that it is suitable and that you have selected a clear escape route;
- no one (including third parties) is within two tree lengths of the tree being felled;
- the operator has a secure foothold, an escape route and as clear a site as possible.

Avoid working alone with a chainsaw. Where this is not possible, work out how you will raise the alarm if something goes wrong, eg mobile phone pre-set button.

Combined chain brake and front hand guard

Hand/eye/ear defender symbols

Guide bar (a cover should be fitted when transporting)

Exhaust (directed away from the operator)

On/off switch

Throttle trigger lockout

Chain with low-kickback characteristics

Chain catcher

Anti-vibration mounts

Rear chain breakage guard

Chainsaws

Use the following checklists to safeguard operators. It is essential for their safe use that chainsaws are properly maintained and correctly stored.

Check that:

- the on/off switch is clearly marked;
- the side plate, front and rear hand guards are fitted, in position and in good order, with the chain, guide bar and sprockets and chain catcher undamaged;
- a chain with low kickback characteristics is used;
- the chain is properly sharpened, tensioned and lubricated;
- the chain brake is properly adjusted and working;
- the silencer and anti-vibration mounts are in good working order.

Circular saws

When using circular saws:

- always use push-sticks or log grippers;
- make sure all saw guards, including the riving knife, are in position. Adjust guards as close as possible to the work;
- regularly examine blades for cracks or missing teeth. Do not use any blades which have teeth missing, which are cracked, or which show signs of welded or brazed repairs;
- check that the blade will run at the correct speed, and that it is still sharp and correctly tensioned;
- make sure the saw bench is at a correct height, securely anchored, protected against the weather, and that the drive or power can be disconnected effectively. If it is tractor powered, ensure the PTO guard is fitted and maintained;
- make sure the circular saw is well maintained;
- make sure it has a braking system if the rundown time of the blade after switching off power is greater than ten seconds. This will not be necessary on machines where the blade is fully enclosed while it comes to rest.

Other machinery

- A standard farm tractor will not be suitable for forestry use without substantial modification to protect vulnerable equipment, improve stability, and increase traction.
- Winch tractors must be able to be properly anchored by the use of spades, a winch butt plate or dozer blade. Winching is always better than towing, but if you must use a conventional tractor for towing, then attach the cable to the drawbar in its lowest position and in line with the direction of pull. Never tow across a slope.
- When using log splitters, firmly position the timber before splitting begins, avoid splitting into a knot and never use hands or feet to hold the log in place during the splitting process.
- Log-loading cranes are potentially hazardous to people nearby. The operator must have a good view of the work area, and no one should be within the 'risk zone' (twice the reach of the boom) or on the trailer during loading. Beware of OHPLs.

The chainsaw operator

Never use a chainsaw without the correct PPE – the risk of injury from the chainsaw cannot be controlled adequately in any other way. Provide the following:

- safety helmet – to BS EN 397;
- hearing protection – to BS EN 352–1;
- eye protection – mesh visors to BS EN 1731 or safety glasses to BS EN 166;
- gloves – appropriate gloves are recommended under most circumstances. The type of glove will depend on a risk assessment of the task and the machine. Consider the need for protection from cuts from the chainsaw, thorny material and cold/wet conditions. Where chainsaw protection is required, provide gloves to BS EN 381–7;
- leg protection – to BS EN 381–5. All-round protection is recommended for occasional users, eg in farming;
- chainsaw boots – to BS EN ISO 20345 and bearing a shield depicting a chainsaw to show compliance with BS EN 381–3. For occasional users working on even ground where there is little risk of tripping or snagging on undergrowth or brash, protective gaiters conforming to BS EN 381–9 worn in combination with steel-toe-capped safety boots.

Helmet

Eye protection

Hearing protection

Appropriate gloves

Leg protection and chainsaw boots

- never use a chainsaw while standing in a tree unless you have been properly trained. This requires specialist skills and a competent arboricultural contractor should be used.

Work from ladders

Do not use a chainsaw when working from a ladder. Chainsaws require both hands to be operated safely and working from a ladder requires one hand to hold the ladder to maintain a steady position. Ladders are normally only used as a means of access into the crown of the tree.

Ropes and harnesses

Using a chainsaw from a rope and harness requires special skills. This should only be done by people who have obtained the relevant certificates of competence or national competence award for:

- climbing trees and performing aerial rescue;
- using a chainsaw from a rope and harness.

Management of tree stocks

Remember that you need to consider public safety as part of an overall approach to tree management. Particular attention will need to be paid to trees where there is frequent public access, for example along popular footpaths or beside busy roads.

Also provide:

- adequate training for the job in hand, including training in how to deal with dangerous situations that can arise during the work, eg hung-up trees or clearance of windblow;
- communication, transport arrangements and location details in case of an accident;
- first-aid arrangements at the site of work.

Working with chainsaws off the ground

Chainsaws should never be used off the ground unless the operator has been adequately trained in safe working techniques. Work off the ground involving the lifting and lowering of people or loads, including work-positioning techniques, will be subject to the requirements of the WAHR and LOLER Regulations. See section 8 'Preventing falls' and section 10 'Workplace transport'.

NB: Rear-handled saws must be used when working on the ground. Top-handled chainsaws are only suitable for use off the ground, by trained and certificated arborists.

Mobile elevating work platforms

When working at height, eg lopping overhanging branches which interfere with fieldwork operations:

- never access branches to be removed by using ladders, grain buckets, or by standing on the top of other machines;
- always use a purpose-built platform such as a mobile elevating work platform (MEWP);
- make sure operators have received adequate training in the safe operation of the platform and the safe use of a chainsaw from the work platform;

Find out more

Tree-climbing operations AFAG401(rev2)
Chainsaws at work INDG317(rev2)
HSE's treework webpages: www.hse.gov.uk/treework
National Tree Safety Group *Common sense risk management of trees: Landowner summary of guidance*

18 COSHH and health

The law

The Control of Substances Hazardous to Health Regulations 2002 (as amended) (COSHH) require that employers assess and control the risks from hazardous substances.

What COSHH covers

Using chemicals or exposure to other hazardous substances at work can make you ill. COSHH covers all substances hazardous to health, including:

- substances used directly in work activities, eg cleaning chemicals, dairy disinfectants, fertilisers, many pesticides and veterinary medicines;
- substances generated during work activities, eg fumes from welding;
- naturally occurring substances, eg grain dust, poultry dust, silo and slurry pit gases;
- biological agents, eg bacteria and fungi.

What COSHH requires

COSHH requires you to:

- assess the risks to health from the hazardous substances used in or created by your work activities;
- decide what precautions are necessary to protect workers;
- prevent or adequately control exposure. Where you can't eliminate exposure, introduce measures to reduce exposure to minimise the risks;
- make sure that control measures are used and properly maintained and that safe working practices are followed;
- carry out health surveillance and monitor workers' health;
- inform, instruct and train employees about the risks and the precautions needed. Adequate supervision is also essential;
- prepare plans to deal with injuries, incidents and emergencies, eg a leakage or spillage of chemicals.

If your general risk assessment has covered hazardous substances you do not need to repeat it.

Prevent exposure

You should first aim to eliminate exposure to hazardous substances. You might:

- change the way you work so that the hazardous substance is not needed or generated, eg don't use corrosive silage additives;
- replace a hazardous substance with a safer alternative, eg use water-based paint rather than solvent-based paint;
- use the hazardous substance in a different form, eg introduce a liquid or wet feed in place of a dusty meal or crumb.

Control exposure

If you have to use the hazardous substance or you can't avoid exposure to a natural product such as dust from grain or poultry, then you must put in place appropriate control measures, including, in order of priority, one or more of the following:

- ways of working that minimise the amount of substance used or produced;
- engineering controls, eg enclosing the process or fitting LEV to remove toxic fume or dust at source;
- minimising how long people are exposed, or how many;
- good housekeeping to minimise accidental contact;
- PPE, eg dust masks, respirators, gloves etc, but never as a replacement for other measures;
- good washing facilities;
- training in the use of engineering controls, good practice, and protective equipment.

Remember that engineering controls protect both the operator and other people in the workplace, while PPE only protects the wearer. *COSHH essentials for farmers* (www.hse.gov.uk/agriculture/resources/coshh/index.htm) gives advice on control measures for a number of common agricultural activities.

Health surveillance

Despite all your efforts to control exposure to hazardous substances, some workers may still experience symptoms of ill health, often later in life. Health surveillance may be necessary to detect early signs of ill health and, in particular, it may be appropriate when workers are exposed to:

- dusts that may cause asthma or other long-term lung disease;
- substances such as solvents that may cause dermatitis;
- sheep dips that contain organophosphorus (OP) compounds.

Health surveillance might include:

- biological or biological effect monitoring, eg blood tests;
- regular checks by a responsible person, eg a trained supervisor could look at workers' hands for signs of dermatitis;
- periodical enquiries to check that there are no symptoms of ill health, eg asking questions about breathing difficulties;
- monitoring the causes of sickness absence, eg if workers are absent from work due to illness, asking whether they or their doctor associated the illness with their work.

Find out more

COSHH Approved Code of Practice L5
Working with substances hazardous to health: A brief guide to COSHH INDG136(rev5)
Controlling exposure to poultry dust: Guidance for employers AIS39
Grain dust EH66

19 Health problems in agriculture

Health problems caused by work can develop unnoticed and, in some cases, may not become apparent until much later in life. You need to be aware of the health risks associated with your work and the signs or symptoms of developing ill health.

You should report any signs of illness to your employer as soon as you become aware of them. Don't be afraid to visit your doctor. Make sure they know what you do for a living so that appropriate treatment can be started as early as possible. Early diagnosis and treatment may prevent your condition from worsening and may even save your life.

Some health problems suffered as a result of work must be reported to HSE (see section 7 'First aid, emergencies and reporting').

Chest problems

The main causes of respiratory disease or chest problems are dusts or chemicals at work. Even being exposed to these for a short time may cause unpleasant irritation or inflammation in the nose, throat or lungs. Longer exposure may lead to more serious problems including asthma and chronic bronchitis.

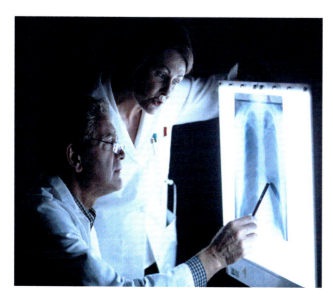

Chest problems may result from breathing in:

- dusts from harvesting or handling grain, mixing animal feedstuffs, feeding animals, handling mouldy hay or bedding in closed buildings used for intensive animal rearing (especially pigs and poultry), and removing waste products from animal or poultry houses;
- vapours (including fumes, gases and aerosols) from slurry, silage, welding fume, some veterinary medicines and disinfectants such as phenols and glutaraldehyde.

Warning signs include irritation/watering of the eyes and nose, blocked stuffy nose, sore throat, cough with or without phlegm, aching muscles or fever, breathlessness, tightness of the chest during work, after work or while doing exercise you could normally cope with, and wheezing.

These symptoms can be short-lived at the time of a job or they may get worse and last longer until they are almost always present. They can be set off by even very small exposures to any substance to which you have become allergic or sensitised. If you smoke, and are also exposed to these substances, you are more likely to develop more serious chest problems.

It is important to protect yourself and your workers. For products that you buy, follow the advice and instructions on the manufacturer's label or data sheet.

Avoid breathing in the harmful substances by:

- using alternative safer substances where possible;
- changing to low dust materials, eg granules or pellets;
- enclosing sources of dust or spray;
- vacuuming spillages instead of sweeping up. Use a high-efficiency filter in the cleaner.

Reduce the amount you breathe in by:

- using LEV, eg when welding;
- using effective filters in tractor or vehicle cabs;
- maintaining filters to the manufacturer's instructions;

- improving ventilation in buildings;
- wearing effective respiratory protective equipment (RPE). Make sure you use the appropriate mask or respirator for dusts, vapours or aerosols.

If you need to wear masks or respirators always adjust the straps so they fit properly. Store them in a clean, dry place and do not hang them from hooks or nails in dirty, dusty areas (see section 23 'Personal protective equipment'). All masks and respirators must be CE-marked.

Zoonoses

Zoonoses are diseases that are passed from animals to humans. Micro-organisms such as bacteria, fungi, parasites and viruses can cause illness by infecting the body when they are breathed in, swallowed, or when they penetrate the skin through small cuts or grazes.

Make sure your COSHH assessment takes zoonoses into account and:

- minimise the risk of infection by keeping stock healthy. Vaccinate where appropriate, eg against enzootic abortion of ewes, avoid contaminating animal drinking water and ask your vet to check stock health regularly;
- avoid or, if this is not possible, reduce contact with animals;
- wear suitable protective clothing such as overalls when handling animals, especially if they are sick, and gloves and a waterproof apron if handling potentially infected material such as products of birth or muck or sewage;
- ensure good personal hygiene. Wash and dry your hands before eating, drinking or smoking;
- immediately wash and dry all cuts and grazes and cover with a waterproof dressing;
- control rats and other vermin that can spread disease.

Consult your vet on likely zoonoses from your animals, but the common ones include:

- orf from sheep or goats, which produces painful pustules on hands, arms and face;
- leptospirosis from rats (Weil's disease) and cattle urine, which causes a feverish illness with headache and can result in meningitis. Early treatment is vital;
- ringworm, which is a fungal disease from many types of livestock;
- enzootic abortion (chlamydia psittaci) from sheep. Pregnant women should not associate or work with ewes during lambing, nor be exposed to soiled clothing contaminated with afterbirths etc as severe illness and miscarriage may result;
- cryptosporidiosis, from a parasite picked up by touching livestock, animal housing, or feed, which can cause diarrhoea in humans, and be particularly severe in young children;
- Lyme disease, from the bite of an infected tick in woodland or grassland. Starts with a rash around the site of the bite and intermittent flu-like symptoms. More serious symptoms affecting the nervous system may develop later. Early diagnosis is essential;
- Q fever from cattle and sheep can also be carried by other mammals, including deer. Leads to acute illness with feverish symptoms but occasionally pneumonia and other complications. There is also a more serious chronic form of Q fever;
- ornithosis (another form of chlamydia psittaci) from birds, which can cause flu-like symptoms in humans, followed by pneumonia.

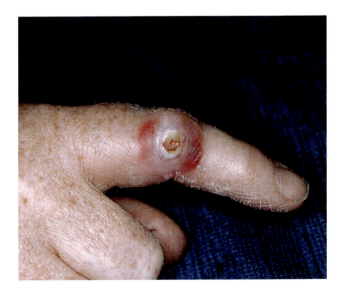

Orf pustule

Diseases transmitted from animals to humans can also affect visitors to your farm, especially children or the elderly. Illness following infection by some virulent forms of E.coli bacterium, eg O26 and O157, may be severe and even fatal. Any ruminant (cattle, sheep, goats and deer) may carry the organism, which can survive for many weeks in faeces or soil. Good personal hygiene is essential (see section 15 'Child and public safety').

Skin problems

The outer layer of the skin, when intact, acts as a barrier to keep moisture in and harmful substances out. Preventing damage will reduce the risk of subsequent problems such as:

- contact dermatitis (or eczema), ie inflammation of the skin due to contact with substances causing irritation or allergy;
- wound infections;
- skin cancers.

Warning signs include dryness, cracking, irritation, itchiness and pain, inflammation and redness, and abnormal growth or discolouration. If you have ever suffered from eczema your skin may be more vulnerable to damage.

The main causes of damage are:

- cuts, punctures or abrasions;
- exposure to cold and wet, leading to dryness and chapping;
- frequent immersion in water, which removes natural oils from the skin;
- exposure to chemicals or to plant materials, including sap;
- overexposure to sunlight, with increased risk of skin cancer.

To avoid skin problems:

- read product labels for information on the precautions you need to take;
- wear suitable gloves when handling chemicals or if damage to your skin is likely;
- wash your hands to remove harmful substances, especially chemical contamination, even if you cannot see it;
- dry your hands thoroughly after washing;
- apply moisturiser regularly after washing and at night;
- wash and dry cuts and grazes and cover with a waterproof dressing;
- treat minor infections immediately.

In sunny weather:

- don't strip off, but keep your top on, especially while you are working in the three or four hours around noon. A wide-brimmed hat will shade the face and head;
- use an effective sunscreen cream or lotion which can provide useful additional protection for parts of the body that are not easy to shade from the sun. Don't forget to reapply, if necessary, throughout the day to maintain protection;
- apply moisturiser regularly after washing and at night to help maintain the outer barrier layer of the skin.

If you notice any changes in warts, moles or skin discolouration then seek your doctor's advice. Always see your doctor if you are concerned about your skin condition, as it is important to treat infections and inflammations properly.

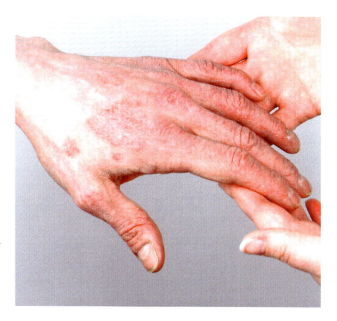

The sap from many plants, including celery, parsnips and primula, can cause skin problems, which may be worse if the skin is exposed to the sun ('phytophotosensitivity'). In most cases, gloves will prevent contact between the sap and the skin so that problems will not recur.

Stress

Stress is the reaction people have to excessive pressure or other types of demand placed on them. Many people in agriculture work under pressure, eg from conflicting demands, too much to do in too little time, or working with inadequately controlled hazards.

The law requires you, as employers, to take action and there are practical things that farming businesses can do to manage the risks associated with work-related stress. For more information on stress see the HSE website: www.hse.gov.uk/stress.

Independent, trained help and information is available from charities such as the Rural Stress Information Network, which co-ordinates a number of local initiatives, Rural Minds, and from befrienders at Samaritans.

You can get more advice on health problems in agriculture from your GP, from HSE's medical inspectors, or from other health and safety professionals, including occupational health doctors and nurses and occupational hygienists.

Find out more

Grain dust EH66
Controlling exposure to poultry dust: Guidance for employers AIS39
Is poultry dust making you ill? INDG426 (pocket card)

20 Pesticides and veterinary medicines

The law

The definition of pesticides includes plant protection products and biocides. European legislation applies to the placing on the market and use of plant protection products (eg agricultural and amenity pesticides). This is implemented in the UK by the Plant Protection Products Regulations 2011 and the Plant Protection Products (Sustainable Use) Regulations 2012.

The Biocidal Products Regulations and the Food and Environment Protection Act 1985 (FEPA) is the relevant UK legislation for the placing on the market and use of biocides (eg rodenticides, disinfectants, wood preservatives etc).

Pesticides may be hazardous substances under the COSHH Regulations.

Veterinary medicines may contain substances that are potentially harmful to human health. The use of these products will also be subject to the COSHH Regulations.

Pesticides

You should only buy pesticides that have been approved for storage and use in the UK. Look for the HSE, MAFF or MAPP approval number on the product's label. Beware of all offers of cheap pesticides, as these may be illegal unapproved products. Lists of approved products can be found on HSE's websites: www.pesticides.gov.uk and www.hse.gov.uk/biocides.

Storing and transporting pesticides

All pesticides should be stored in their original containers with the approved product labels. Never decant pesticides into drinks bottles or other similar containers.

HSE's information sheet AIS16 *Guidance on storing pesticides for farmers and other professional users* sets out the standards for both fixed and mobile stores. All stores should be:

- designed to contain leakage or spillage;
- constructed of non-combustible material;
- secured against unauthorised access.

Practise good store management, including keeping an up-to-date stock record. Keep a copy readily available in the event of an emergency. Always check containers for leakage before removing them from storage. Do not remove leaking containers, but either over-drum or transfer the contents to a sound container. Do not leave stores open when unattended. Supervise all deliveries to make sure that new stock is stored safely and securely.

Never carry pesticides in the cab of a tractor, self-propelled equipment or other vehicle. Use either a:

- vehicle with a bulkhead between the cab and the load compartment;
- secure, leak-proof chemical container; or
- secure cabinet mounted on the outside of the vehicle or on a trailer.

Make sure you lock the vehicle or cabinet whenever you are not in sight of it.

Use pesticides properly

The decision to use pesticides should not be taken lightly and should form part of a thorough risk assessment. You may need expert help to make the right decision and (if you do decide to use a pesticide) to choose the right product.

Failure to use pesticides correctly can put people and the environment at risk. The aquatic environment is very sensitive to pesticide contamination. Plan the use of pesticides carefully and make sure that you put the appropriate controls in place before you start, including what to do if anything goes wrong. Take special care when applying pesticides near to water. You may need to complete a local environmental risk assessment for pesticides (LERAP).

- Always read and make sure you understand the

instructions on the label and in any safety data sheet (SDS) or leaflet supplied with the product. Failure to follow these instructions may be an offence and may lead to prosecution.
- Make sure you use any PPE identified in the instructions.
- Only spray when weather conditions are suitable to reduce spray drift.
- Try to avoid walking through treated areas.
- Do not eat, drink or smoke when applying pesticides.
- Wash hands before taking a rest break.
- Do not use faulty application equipment. All equipment should be maintained to a high standard to prevent leakage and calibrated to ensure accurate application.
- Do not overfill sprayer tanks and secure all caps and lids before use.
- After use, clean all equipment inside and out, preferably before leaving the treatment area. Return any unused pesticide to the store or dispose of it safely and legally.
- Advice on the disposal of waste pesticides, including

packaging (containers, closures and seals) and pesticide washings can be obtained from the Environment Agency: www.environment-agency.gov.uk.

■ Finally, keep a record of all pesticide use.

The National Sprayer Testing Scheme (NSTS), run by the Agricultural Engineers Association (AEA), is an independent voluntary inspection and testing scheme that can be used for a variety of application equipment.

Everyone who uses pesticides must be competent and have received adequate guidance, instruction or training for their correct use. In some cases (eg use of a plant protection product authorised for professional use), the user must hold an appropriate 'specified certificate' (currently a certificate of competence), or work under the direct supervision of someone who holds such a certificate. However, all regular users of pesticides at work are advised to receive formal training and are encouraged to participate in continuous professional development.

Veterinary medicines including sheep dips

When it is necessary to administer veterinary medicines to livestock, effective control measures will be required to reduce the risks to human health, for example:

■ Select a less hazardous veterinary product, eg a water-based vaccine instead of an oil-based one. This may be less likely to cause harm if you accidentally inject yourself.
■ Use a safer application system, eg a pour-on or injectable product may be safer for the operator than plunge dipping for sheep.
■ Provide effective engineering controls, eg properly designed dipping facilities with splash screens around the dip bath, to reduce operator contamination from splashing.
■ Provide facilities to make sure animals are properly restrained. This will make injections and other treatments easier.
■ Use injection equipment incorporating needle guards and disinfection devices to reduce the risk of needlestick injuries or contamination from dirty needles.
■ Make sure operators are properly trained and competent to safely use the product. Work with veterinary medicines should only be carried out by competent people who have received adequate instruction, information and training.

Under the Veterinary Medicines Regulations it is an offence to use sheep dip unless this is done by, or under the supervision and in the presence of, a person who holds a nationally recognised certificate of competence in the safe use of sheep dips.

■ Dispose of any surplus concentrate or dilute product safely. Careless use or disposal of sheep dips creates a risk to aquatic life, so use, store and dispose of any dip properly – not into watercourses or soakaways.
■ Dispose of used syringes and needles in a sharps bin.
■ Always follow the label or package instructions carefully, especially those relating to PPE.
■ Wash off splashes from the skin and clothing immediately, and wash before eating, drinking or smoking. Don't work among freshly treated animals if you could be contaminated, unless you are wearing PPE.
■ Follow any emergency measures recommended by the manufacturer; eg with oil-based vaccines, if you inject yourself seek prompt medical attention.
■ Report all suspected cases of poisoning or other adverse reactions so they can be thoroughly investigated.

To report a suspected adverse reaction to veterinary medicines in animals or humans, contact the Veterinary Medicines Directorate (VMD) under the Suspected Adverse Reaction Surveillance Scheme (SARSS). Contact VMD at: www.vmd.gov.uk.

Storing veterinary medicines and other chemicals

You need to provide a suitable store for veterinary medicines. Other hazardous substances such as dairy detergents and disinfectants should also be stored safely and securely where they cannot harm the environment or children.

Store securely all medicines and application equipment such as syringes and needles, where children cannot get at them.

Check that containers of potentially hazardous substances are locked away when not needed for immediate use, in an area:

■ safe from accidental damage and children, vermin or birds;
■ that is fireproof for 30 minutes;
■ able to contain spillages, with protected drains if they might be polluted.

Keep records of what is in the store in case of fire.

Find out more

Code of practice for using plant protection products (available from www.pesticides.gov.uk)
LERAP: Horizontal boom sprayers (www.pesticides.gov.uk)
Guidance on storing pesticides for farmers and other professional users AIS16(rev1)
Sheep dipping: Advice for farmers and others involved in dipping sheep AIS41
Veterinary medicines: Safe use by farmers and other animal handlers AS31(rev2)
For information on certificates of competence in sheep dipping and veterinary medicines see www.nptc.org.uk

21 Manual handling

Manual handling includes lifting, carrying, putting down, pushing, pulling, moving or supporting a load by hand or using other bodily force. It is not just the weight of the load that can cause injury: the size, shape, available grip, the way you carry the load, where you have to carry it, and how often you have to do the task all play a part.

Many workers in the industry suffer from a variety of 'musculoskeletal disorders' (MSDs) as a result of poor manual handling techniques, or through other tasks which involve repetitive movements, excessive force, unusual postures, or from badly organised working practices.

These can include muscle injuries, sprains or strains, back pain, sciatica, hernias, arthritis, or swelling of the hand, wrist, forearm, elbow and shoulder ('work-related upper limb disorders' or WRULDs). People may not fully recover from these, affecting their ability to carry out any manual work in the future. So, plan your handling tasks properly.

Can you avoid manual handling?

Consider whether you have to move the load manually at all. If possible, eliminate manual handling completely, for example:

- fully mechanise the task. A move to big bales, or fertiliser in big bags, eliminates manual handling because they are so large or heavy they can only be moved by machine;
- introduce feed-handling systems incorporating bulk storage bins and distribution pipes to eliminate the handling of feed compounds;
- use other mechanised systems to eliminate the filling, carrying and tipping of small feed bags or sacks.

Remember, the Regulations do not set specific requirements such as weight limits. Consider the task, the load, individual capability, and the working conditions.

Assess the risks

If you cannot avoid manual handling, look at the risks from your handling operations. You do not have to look at every task in detail – if the load is less than about 25 kg, easily gripped close to the body, and the working conditions are good (eg indoors, with a level floor and plenty of space) the risk of injury to most people will be low. Instead, focus on the tasks with the greatest risks.

Use HSE's *Manual handling assessment charts (MAC tool)* to help you identify problem areas, eg loads that:

- weigh over 25 kg or are difficult to grip or handle because of their size or shape;
- need frequent lifting or lowering, or carrying over long distances;
- are difficult to manoeuvre, and/or involve twisting or lifting above shoulder height or from the floor.

Reduce the risk of injury

If you cannot eliminate the risk completely, look at how you can reduce it to an acceptable level, for example:

- use mechanical assistance and/or lifting aids. Materials handlers, forklift trucks, sack trucks, trolleys for bales, workshop cranes, drum cradles etc can all reduce the amount of effort involved and reduce the risk of injury. Workers are likely to need training to use these devices safely;
- change to smaller, lighter unit sizes, eg use feed blocks or feed bags weighing 25 kg or less to make lifting and carrying easier;
- reduce lifting or carrying distances by providing mechanical or other ways to move goods;
- find improved ways of handling.

For animals, use properly designed cattle races and crushes or sheep turnover crates to reduce the risks during animal handling and husbandry tasks (see section 16 'Handling livestock' for more information).

For containers:

- sharp edges, wrap a protective layer around the sharp edge;
- liquid or flowing contents, use smaller containers which can be filled so that the contents do not move around, changing the weight distribution.

Practical tips for safe lifting

Think before lifting/handling

Plan the lift. Can handling aids be used? Where is the load going to be placed? Will help be needed with the load? Remove obstructions such as discarded wrapping materials.

Adopt a stable position

The feet should be apart with one leg slightly forward to maintain balance (alongside the load, if it is on the ground). Be prepared to move your feet during the lift to maintain stability and avoid tight clothing or unsuitable footwear, which may make this difficult.

Get a good hold

Where possible, the load should be hugged as close as possible to the body. This may be better than gripping it tightly with hands only.

Posture is important

At the start of the lift, slight bending of the back, hips and knees is preferable to fully flexing the back (stooping) or fully flexing the hips and knees (squatting).

Don't flex the back any further while lifting

This can happen if the legs begin to straighten before starting to raise the load.

Keep the load close to the waist

The load should be kept close to the body for as long as possible while lifting. Keep the heaviest side of the load next to the body. If a close approach to the load is not possible, try to slide it towards the body before attempting to lift it.

Avoid twisting the back or leaning sideways, especially while your back is bent

Shoulders should be kept level and facing in the same direction as the hips. Turning by moving the feet is better than twisting and lifting at the same time.

Keep your head up when handling

Look ahead, not down at the load, once it has been held securely.

Move smoothly

The load should not be jerked or snatched as this can make it harder to keep control and can increase the risk of injury.

Don't lift or handle more than can be easily managed

There is a difference between what people can lift and what they can **safely** lift. If in doubt, seek advice or get help.

Put down, then adjust

If precise positioning of the load is nescessary, put it down first, then slide it into the desired position.

Don't forget to look at working conditions:

- Allow people to work at their own pace where possible.
- Build adequate rests or pauses into the work.
- Check that floors and access routes are level, well lit, not slippery, unobstructed, and there is enough space to move the load.
- Workers should be warm but not too hot as this may increase the risk of heat stress.

If particularly large or awkward loads cannot be moved with mechanical assistance, you will need to arrange help:

- Discuss and plan the work first and get everyone to work together, eg a team lift.
- Make sure one person is in charge, giving clear, unhurried instructions.
- Provide PPE for hands and feet, and other protective clothing where necessary.

Where manual handling tasks remain and cannot be avoided make sure that workers know how to use the correct lifting techniques and provide training to enable them to do this.

Remember:

A good handling technique or training in safe lifting is no substitute for other risk-reduction steps such as improving the task, load or working environment; or providing mechanical handling or lifting aids. Good technique requires both training and practice. Training is available from various sources, including training groups, colleges and organisations such as Lantra Awards.

Work-related upper limb disorders

If workers suffer from pain, numbness or tingling in the hands, aching or shooting pains up the arms, difficulty in gripping, or swelling over a joint, they may be suffering from a WRULD. Typical work that causes these symptoms includes working on grading lines, on inspection tables, on root harvesters, or processing poultry.

To reduce the risks, consider these measures:

- Change the work area and provide adjustable seats and work tables at the right height.
- Select tools with handles and ergonomic design features to suit the hand.
- Allow new workers to build up their work rate gradually.
- Rotate jobs to allow for a variety of postures and activities.
- Build short and frequent breaks into the job.
- Encourage early reporting of symptoms so that action can be taken.

Find out more

For more information on manual handling visit:
www.hse.gov.uk/msd

22 Noise and vibration

The law

The Control of Noise at Work Regulations 2005 (the Noise Regulations) aim to reduce the risk of hearing damage caused by exposure to loud noise. Employers are required to assess the risks, take action to reduce noise exposure at certain action and limit values, provide workers with hearing protection where noise cannot be reduced by other methods, and make sure the legal limits on noise exposure are not exceeded. They must provide their workers with information, instruction and training and, in certain circumstances, carry out health surveillance. Employees and the self-employed also have legal duties to protect themselves against noise.

The Control of Vibration at Work Regulations 2005 aim to protect workers from the risks to health from exposure to vibration. They apply to both employers and the self-employed.

Noise

Exposure to high noise levels can cause permanent hearing damage, often without the sufferer being aware of it until it is too late. It may lead to tinnitus (ringing in the ears) or deafness. Noise can also be a safety hazard at work, interfering with communication and making warnings harder to hear.

Typical noise levels

The diagram gives examples of how noisy some agricultural activities are.

What are the noise action and limit values?

Noise is measured in decibels. The action levels in the Noise Regulations are defined in terms of daily noise exposure (the daily average) and peak noise exposure (sudden noises).

- The lower exposure action values are 80 dB for daily exposure and 135 dB for peak noise.
- The upper exposure action levels are 85 dB for daily exposure and 137 dB for peak noise.
- The limits, which must not be exceeded, are 87 dB for daily exposure and 140 dB for peak noise.

Remember:

- Exposure to many different sources of noise (eg tractors, chainsaws, grain dryers and guns) has a cumulative effect and can cause damage, even though you may only be exposed to a single source for short periods of time.
- Intensively housed animals can create noise levels above the action levels. Pigs at feeding time can create levels of 100 dB or more.

Controlling noise

Protection against noise is best achieved by controlling it at source. Get noise levels assessed by a competent person and keep a record. To reduce exposure:

- choose quiet machines or processes when selecting production methods or new machines. Get the supplier to specify noise levels at the operators' positions;
- enclose noisy machines or processes with sound-insulating panels, or put them in separate rooms. Fit silencers on exhaust systems;
- reduce the need to work in intensive animal housing at feeding times by changing the feeding regime, putting controls etc on the outside or in a protected area, or doing other jobs when the animals are fed and contented;

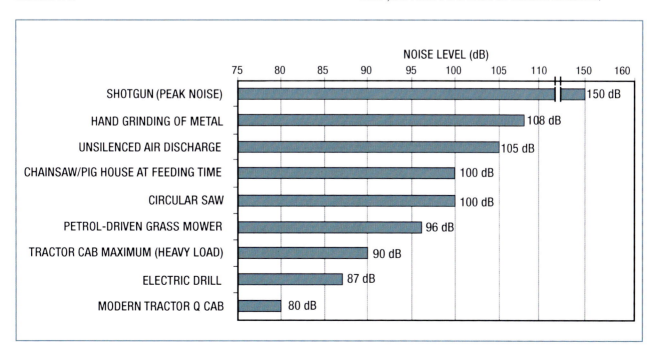

NOISE LEVEL (dB)

SHOTGUN (PEAK NOISE)	150 dB
HAND GRINDING OF METAL	108 dB
UNSILENCED AIR DISCHARGE	105 dB
CHAINSAW/PIG HOUSE AT FEEDING TIME	100 dB
CIRCULAR SAW	100 dB
PETROL-DRIVEN GRASS MOWER	96 dB
TRACTOR CAB MAXIMUM (HEAVY LOAD)	90 dB
ELECTRIC DRILL	87 dB
MODERN TRACTOR Q CAB	80 dB

■ reduce the duration of exposure by job rotation, providing a noise refuge, or arranging the work so that no one needs to be in the noisy area;

■ provide workers with hearing protection if they ask for it and their exposure is between the lower and upper exposure action values;

■ where exposures reach 85 dB or higher, mark these areas as 'hearing protection zones', with signs to indicate that hearing protection must be worn, and make sure everyone entering these zones wears hearing protection;

■ get operators in noisy areas to wear hearing protection, and tell them about the risks to their hearing. If any of your workers think their hearing is being affected, suggest they take medical advice and consider the need for regular hearing checks as part of health surveillance.

Remember:

■ Hearing protection should be the last resort to control noise exposure. Whether you use ear muffs, plugs or inserts, you will only get the assumed protection if they are in good condition, the correct size and worn properly.

■ To be effective, you need to wear hearing protection all the time in noisy places. If you leave it off for even short periods, the amount of protection will be severely limited and it will not protect your hearing.

■ Maintenance of machines and changes in work methods can affect noise levels. Loose panels or unbalanced rotating parts can contribute to noise and vibration.

Vibration

Repeated or prolonged use of vibrating tools such as chainsaws, brush cutters or grinders can lead to hand-arm vibration syndrome (HAVS), a group of diseases including vibration white finger, nerve, muscle or joint damage. Warning signs include tingling or numbness in the fingers, fingers turning white in cold or damp conditions, followed by throbbing and flushing.

Whole-body vibration (WBV) is the vibration and shock you feel when you sit or stand on a vehicle or machine travelling over rough ground or along a track, or the vibration when you work near powerful machinery such as milling machinery. Shocks can occur, eg when driving over bumps or potholes.

Remember:

■ Use the right machine for the job, eg chainsaws designed for low vibration, with heated handles or with anti-vibration mounts, tractors with suspended axles or chassis for transport work.

■ Maintain equipment correctly, eg anti-vibration mountings on chainsaws.

■ Start with warm hands, keep them warm, and take regular breaks.

■ Make full use of the tractor seat position and suspension adjustments.

■ Travel at an appropriate speed for the ground conditions, and choose the right course to avoid ruts etc.

■ Maintain traffic routes as smooth as possible and free of bumps and ruts.

■ Avoid high levels of vibration and/or prolonged exposure for older workers, those with existing back problems, young people and pregnant women.

■ See whether you can restrict exposure by limiting the amount of time workers use vibrating equipment.

See also section 11 'Selecting and using work equipment'.

Exposure to WBV at low levels is unlikely on its own to cause back pain, but it can aggravate existing back injuries, which may cause pain. There are many causes of back pain other than WBV, which must be adequately controlled. The most likely cause of back pain should be tackled first (see section 21 'Manual handling').

Find out more

Whole-body vibration in agriculture AIS20(rev2)
Hand-arm vibration at work: A brief guide INDG175(rev3)
Control back-pain risks from whole-body vibration: Advice for employers INDG242(rev1)
Noise at work: A brief guide to controlling the risks INDG362(rev2)
Noise: Don't lose your hearing (pocket card) INDG363(rev2)
Drive away bad backs: Advice for mobile machine operators and drivers INDG404

23 Personal protective equipment

PPE includes coveralls, eye protection, footwear, gloves,

The law

The Personal Protective Equipment at Work Regulations 1992 (as amended) require that PPE provided for use at work must be made to an appropriate standard and must be CE-marked.

safety helmets and wet weather clothing. Hearing protection and RPE provided for most work situations are not covered by these Regulations because other regulations apply to them. However, these items need to be compatible with any other PPE provided and are briefly covered in this section. Your health and safety and that of workers can depend on it.

When selecting PPE, remember:

■ You need to consider and introduce other means of protection first. Provide PPE as a last resort after taking all other reasonably practicable measures.
■ Engineering controls provide long-term solutions and are often cheaper than providing, replacing, maintaining and storing PPE.
■ Controls at source protect all workers in the area, while PPE only protects the wearer.
■ It is essential to involve the workers themselves in the selection process, as they often have detailed knowledge of the way things work, or are done, which can help you.

Also, make sure that PPE:

■ is effective and gives adequate protection against the hazards in the workplace, eg for handling acids do the gloves resist acid penetration?
■ is readily available for use;
■ is suitable and matches the wearer, the task and the working environment, so that it does not get in the way of the job being done or cause any discomfort;
■ does not introduce any additional risks, eg limit visibility or cause heat stress;
■ is compatible with any other PPE that has to be worn; eg safety spectacles may interfere with the fit of respirators;
■ is checked before use and cleaned, maintained and stored in accordance with the manufacturer's instructions.

So they can use the equipment effectively, workers should be given suitable information, instruction and training.

Remember that employers are not permitted to charge their employees for PPE provided for use only at work.

Types of PPE you can use

Eyes
Hazards: chemical or metal splash, dust, projectiles, gas and vapour, radiation
Options: safety spectacles, goggles, faceshields, visors

Head
Hazards: impact from falling or flying objects, risk of head bumping, hair entanglement in machinery, chemical drips or splash, climate or temperature
Options: a range of head protection including hard hats, safety helmets and bump caps

Ears
Hazards: noise – a combination of sound level and duration of exposure, very high-level sounds are a hazard even with short duration
Options: earplugs, earmuffs, semi-insert/canal caps

Hands and arms
Hazards: abrasion, temperature extremes, cuts and punctures, impact, chemicals, electric shock, vibration, biological agents and prolonged immersion in water
Options: gloves, gloves with a cuff, gauntlets and sleeving that covers part or all of the arm

Feet and legs
Hazards: wet, hot and cold conditions, electrostatic build-up, slipping, cuts and punctures, falling objects, heavy loads, metal and chemical splash, vehicles
Options: safety boots and shoes with protective toe caps, and penetration-resistant, mid-sole wellington boots, specific footwear, eg chainsaw boots

Lungs
Hazards: dusts, fibres, mists, fumes, micro-organisms (bioaerosols), gases, vapours and oxygen-deficient atmospheres
Options: disposable filtering facepieces or respirators, half- or full-face respirators, air-fed helmets, breathing apparatus

Whole body
Hazards: heat, chemical or metal splash, spray from pressure leaks or spray guns, contaminated dust, impact or penetration, excessive wear or entanglement of own clothing
Options: conventional or disposable overalls, boiler suits, specialist protective clothing, eg chemical suits, high-visibility clothing

Respiratory protective equipment

Work activities may result in harmful substances contaminating the air in the form of dusts, fibres, mists, fumes, micro-organisms (bioaerosols), gases or vapours, for example:

■ cutting a material, eg stone, concrete or wood;
■ handling a dusty material, eg grain or poultry litter/ manure;
■ using a liquid containing volatile solvents, eg paints.

Workers may also need to work in areas where oxygen levels are low, eg confined spaces such as a silo or tank.

RPE is designed to protect the wearer from these hazards.

When can RPE be used?

■ When you might still breathe in contaminated air, despite other controls you have in place, eg extraction systems.
■ When there is short-term or infrequent exposure and using other controls is impractical.
■ While you are putting other controls in place.
■ When you need to provide RPE for safe exit in an emergency.
■ When you need to provide RPE for emergency work or when there is a temporary failure of controls.
■ When emergency rescue by trained personnel is necessary.

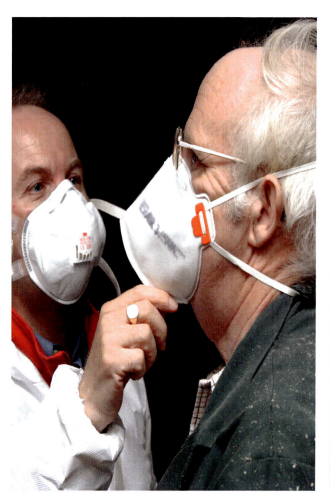

How do I choose the right RPE?

RPE should be right for the:

■ wearer
■ task
■ environment

To help you find the right RPE, you can either:

■ look at the *COSHH essentials* guidance sheets (see 'Find out more') to see if any cover your work task and recommend a type of RPE;
■ look at HSG53 (see 'Find out more') and follow its approach to selection;
■ use the online RPE Selector Tool (see 'Find out more'), developed jointly by the Scottish Centre for Healthy Working Lives and HSE.

Using your RPE

To ensure your RPE works, you should make sure:

■ the chosen RPE fits and is suitable for the task and the wearer;
■ you conduct fit tests for each wearer, for each piece of tight-fitting RPE they use;
■ the RPE works with other protective equipment the user wears;
■ the wearers are trained to use it and are supervised;
■ the RPE is checked before use and cleaned, maintained and stored in accordance with the manufacturer's instructions.

Respirators relying on filtration for their efficiency should never be used to provide protection in oxygen-deficient atmospheres.

See section 13 'Workplace safety and welfare' for advice on work in confined spaces. RPE with an independent air supply, eg breathing apparatus, will be necessary for such work.

Emergency equipment

Careful selection, maintenance and regular and realistic operator training is needed for equipment for use in emergencies, like compressed-air escape breathing apparatus, respirators and safety ropes or harnesses.

Find out more

Personal Protective Equipment at Work Regulations *1992 (as amended). Guidance on Regulations* L25
Personal protective equipment (PPE) at work: A brief guide INDG174
Respiratory protective equipment at work: A practical guide HSG53
Noise at work: A brief guide to controlling the risks INDG362(rev2)
COSHH essentials guidance sheets online at www.hse. gov.uk/pubns/guidance/index.htm
RPE Selector Tool online at www.healthyworkinglives. com/advice/minimising-workplace-risks/rpe

Agriculture news

An easy way to stay up to date with health and safety news in agriculture

Stay up to date with the latest health and safety news and information on agriculture via a free regular email bulletin, or an RSS feed.

Agriculture eBulletins

eBulletins are issued periodically and provide brief information on a number of topics or issues, each linking to more detailed articles on our website.

Register at www.hse.gov.uk/agriculture/ebulletins.htm

Agriculture RSS newsfeed

All the latest news relating to agriculture in HSE is available through this newsfeed. Subscribe to it through your preferred reader, or find out more about newsfeeds at http://news.hse.gov.uk/category/agriculture/feed

Visit HSE's agriculture website: www.hse.gov.uk/agriculture

Further information

For information about health and safety visit
https://books.hse.gov.uk or http://www.hse.gov.uk.
You can view HSE guidance online and order priced
publications from the website. HSE priced publications
are also available from bookshops.

To report inconsistencies or inaccuracies in this guidance email:
commissioning@wlt.com.

British Standards can be obtained in PDF or hard copy formats
from BSI: http://shop.bsigroup.com or by contacting BSI
Customer Services for hard copies only Tel: 0846 086 9001
email: cservices@bsigroup.com.

The Stationery Office publications are available from
The Stationery Office, PO Box 29, Norwich NR3 1GN
Tel: 0333 202 5070 Fax: 0333 202 5080.
E-mail:customer.services@tso.co.uk Website: www.tso.co.uk.
They are also available from bookshops.

Statutory Instruments can be viewed free of charge at
www.legislation.gov.uk where you can also search for
changes to legislation.